A guide to the most common flora and fauna encountered in Seychelles, including hiking trails for the inner island group

Christophe Mason-Parker

JOHN BEAUFOY PUBLISHING

First published in the United Kingdom in 2022 by John Beaufoy Publishing,
11 Blenheim Court, 316 Woodstock Road, Oxford OX2 7NS, England
www.johnbeaufoy.com

10 9 8 7 6 5 4 3 2 1

ISBN 978-1-913679-28-6

Edited and indexed by Krystyna Mayer
Designed by Nigel Partridge
Cartography by William Smuts
Project management by Rosemary Wilkinson

Printed and bound in Malaysia by Times Offset (M) Sdn Bhd

Photo Credits

All photos by Christophe Mason-Parker except:
p.15 Sheath-tailed Bat, Rachel Bristol; p.19 Amur Falcon x 2, Adrian Skerrett; p.21 Barn Owl, Adrian Skerrett; p.27 Seychelles White-eye, Pierre-Andre Adam; p.31 Tropical Shearwater, Dillys Pouponeau; p.33 Red-tailed Tropicbird, Matthew Morgan; p.35 Roseate Tern, Matthew Morgan; p.43 Sanderling, Adrian Skerrett; p.47 Seychelles Black Mud Terrapin, MCSS; p.47 Seychelles Yellow-bellied Mud Turtle, Laura & Bobby Bok; p.49 Abbot's Day Gecko, Martin Van Rooyen; p.55 Burrowing Skink, Laura & Bobby Bok; p.55 Bauer's Burrowing Skink, Laura & Bobby Bok; p.55 Brahminy Blind Snake, Laura & Bobby Bok; p.59 Thomasset'S Frog, Laura & Bobby Bok; p.59 Seychelles Pygmy Frog, Laura & Bobby Bok; p.59 Silhouette Palm Frog, ICS; p.61 Little Praslin Caecilian, Charles Morel; p.67 Aldabra Banded Snail, Martin Van Rooyen; p.79 Giant Centipede, Laura & Bobby Bok; p.81 Tailess Whipscorpion, Laura & Bobby Bok; p.87 Phantom Flutterer, Laura & Bobby Bok; p.89 Seychelles Winged Stick Insect, Laura & Bobby Bok; p.109 Giant-leave Fig, Charles Morel; p.109 Pisonia, Cheryl Sanchez; p.109 Wright's Gardenia x 2, Dillys Pouponeau; p.121 Dillenia, Charles Morel; p.121 Northia, Charles Morel; p.127 Balfour's Pandanus x 2, Charles Morel; p.129 Jellyfish Tree x 2, Charles Morel; p.131 Tropicbird Orchid, Charles Morel; p.131 Wild Vanilla, Charles Morel.

CONTENTS

INTRODUCTION

Seychelles is rich in biodiversity and supports many species that are found nowhere else on Earth. It is home to the western Indian Ocean's last remaining species of flightless bird, the world's biggest population of giant tortoises and the largest nut on the planet. Visitors to the islands have the opportunity to explore a wide variety of habitats and encounter species that have evolved in isolation over thousands of years. From the coastal plateaux and mid-altitude forests of the granitic islands, to the tidal lagoons and coral reefs of the coralline islands, the natural wonders of Seychelles will not cease to amaze.

This book is the perfect companion for anyone with an interest in the flora and fauna of the Seychelles islands. Whether you are an avid nature enthusiast, a regular hiker or simply looking to identify the bird that you saw outside your window, it provides you with everything you need to know. Including photographs of more than 200 species of plant and animal, with descriptions, advice on where they can be found, and their conservation status, there is useful information about the different islands, as well as on popular hiking trails.

Divided into three parts, with an initial introduction to Seychelles, background information on Seychelles and the practicalities are covered first.

The second part comprises a guide to the wildlife of Seychelles. It features the most common species of flora and fauna to be found in the archipelago, each with a colour photograph and a description of the species, including its common, scientific and local names (the latter in parentheses), size, distribution, behaviour and status. The guide is

 The stunning Madame Zabre Beach on Desroches.

by no means comprehensive and apart from species that are commonly encountered, the focus is on those that are endemic to Seychelles or are likely to be of particular interest to readers. Marine species are outside the scope of this title, and anyone wishing to read about the flora and fauna of Seychelles' marine environment should consult *The Underwater Guide to Seychelles* and other publications on the subject (see Further Reading, p. 192, for details).

The third section features some of the most popular walks and hiking trails in the Seychelles granitic islands. Covering five islands, the list represents only a small fraction of the trails to be found, but does include something to interest most people.

GEOGRAPHY

The 115 islands of the Republic of Seychelles are located in the western Indian Ocean, north-east of Madagascar. Spread out across a vast swathe of ocean at 4–10 degrees south of the Equator, tiny, low-lying coral atolls and spectacular, mist-covered peaks rise out of the turquoise Indian Ocean. With a dramatic landscape, a vibrant culture and a rich flora and fauna both above and below the water, the islands of Seychelles offer visitors an experience of a lifetime. Although the land mass of Seychelles amounts to only 455km^2, the oceanic Exclusive Economic Zone (EEZ) is far greater, at 1.374 million square kilometres. As a biodiversity hotspot, Seychelles offers an incredibly varied experience for wildlife lovers, with many island endemics easily accessible a few minutes from human habitation.

The Seychelles islands are commonly separated into two distinct groups – the

Ile aux Vaches, one of the inner granitic islands.

The densely populated north-east coast of Mahé.

inner and outer islands. The inner islands are home to more than 90 per cent of the human population and are most frequently visited by tourists. This island group sits on the Seychelles plateau and includes 41 granitic islands, alongside the coralline islands of Bird and Denis.

The Seychelles granitic islands are the only oceanic granitic island group in the world, and were once part of the supercontinent of Gondwana. They were formed 65 million years ago and remained in isolation above sea level, allowing for the evolution of a variety of endemic species.

Mahé, Praslin and La Digue are the most developed islands, where the majority of the population of 98,000 people resides. The Seychellois are a proud and cosmopolitan people, made up of mixed ethnicities from Africa, Asia and Europe. There is also a significant number of foreign workers in the tourism, construction and fisheries industries.

West and south of the inner islands are the outer coralline islands, which are distributed across the vast EEZ of Seychelles. Furthest to the west, the raised coralline islands of Aldabra atoll, Cosmoledo atoll and Astove are situated closer to northern Madagascar than they are to Mahé. Those islands were created when reef-building corals were forced upwards, and during their history they have been submerged and resurfaced a number of times. In recent years the islands of Astove and Cosmoledo have opened up to low-impact nature tourism, while the UNESCO World Heritage Site of Aldabra atoll, which is managed by the Seychelles Islands Foundation, is accessible primarily to cruise ships, but with excursions restricted to only certain parts of the atoll.

The remaining coralline islands, including the Farquhar and the Amirantes groups, Platte and Cöetivy islands, were more recently formed and for the most part are less than 3m above sea level. Some of these islands support large colonies of seabirds, but tend to host fewer endemic species than the granitic islands. Many of the islands were

Picard, the third largest of the islands that make up Aldabra Atoll.

heavily exploited in the past, especially for mining of guano and production of copra (coconut plantations), and their terrestrial habitats were altered significantly in the process. In addition to seabird populations, the coralline islands also host important nesting beaches for Hawksbill and Green Turtles.

HISTORICAL BACKGROUND

Although Seychelles is a young nation, its history is fascinating. The archipelago is recorded as having been discovered in 1501 by the Portuguese explorer João de Nova. However, it is believed that traders passed through the islands much earlier. Despite these first visits to the islands' shores, they remained uninhabited until 1770, when a group of French settlers arrived, bringing with them slaves from Africa and India. Very quickly, the colonists established a spice industry, growing cloves, nutmeg and cinnamon.

Over the next 45 years the French continued to rule over Seychelles, until in 1814, amid the upheavals caused by the French revolution, Seychelles became a colony of the British Empire. Soon after, the abolition of slavery lead to an influx of freed slaves, who provided a much-needed workforce for the expansion of the coconut plantations. Despite being a British colony, the islands' French influence remained, and today French is still one of the three official languages, the others being English and Seychellois Creole. The twentieth century brought dramatic changes to Seychelles. As the market for coconut and vanilla dried up, attention turned to the archipelago's other natural resources. Political change was also in the air, with the election of the first legislative council in 1948. By 1964 two political parties had formed. One was the socialist Seychelles People's United Party (SPUP), the other the Seychelles Democratic Party (SDC), which wanted to keep close ties with Britain. In 1970, James Mancham, the leader of the SDC, was elected as Chief Minister of Seychelles.

Finally, on 29 June 1976, and with the support of both political parties, Seychelles became an independent nation, with James Mancham as its first president. Only a year later, however, while Mancham was out of the country, the SPUP staged an armed coup and Seychelles became a single-party socialist state with France Albert René as president. This political situation remained in place for the next 16 years, despite several unsuccessful coups attempting to remove René. Then, in 1991, Mancham returned to Seychelles and a multi-party state was recognized once again. René remained in office until 2004, when he retired and handed over to the then Vice-President, James Alix Michel. The SPUP remained in power until 2020, rebranding to become the United Seychelles (US) party in 2018. However, in October 2020, Wavel Ramkalawan of the Linyon Demokratik Seselwa (LDS) won the presidential election with 54.9 per cent of the votes, and this marked the first peaceful transition of power between political parties since the nation's independence.

CLIMATE

Seychelles is hot and humid, with a near-constant temperature that averages between 24° C (75 °F) and 32° C (89° F). The warm, tropical climate is marked by two distinct seasons, named after the direction of the prevailing winds: the north-west monsoon and the south-east monsoon. From November to March, the north-west monsoon brings variable wind speeds and heavy rain, particularly between December and February. This is the best time of year to search for frogs in the forests of Mahé and Silhouette, although conditions can sometimes be difficult underfoot. October also marks the start of the period when Eurasian bird migrants arrive on the islands.

The south-east monsoon, which lasts from May to September, is cooler and drier with strong winds, leading to rough seas that can sometimes make sea crossings between

Silhouette Island remains densely forested.

islands uncomfortable. Cold upwellings bring plankton to coastal waters, and during July and August sea temperatures often drop to around 25° C (77° F). The changeovers between the two monsoons (March/April and October/November) are categorized by periods of hot, windless weather that usually brings calm seas.

PRACTICALITIES

These are the main practical considerations for visitors to Seychelles.

Language

The official languages of Seychelles are Creole, English and French, with all three widely spoken throughout the islands. Creole is the most commonly spoken language, yet it is not uncommon to hear conversations in which a mix of Creole and English words is used. For those visitors who do not speak any of the three official languages, it is possible to hire tour guides who speak German, Italian and other languages. Nature tours in the special reserves are usually conducted in English or French.

Getting There

The only international airport in Seychelles is located on Mahé and is visited by a number of international airlines. At the time of going to print, there are connections through Ethiopia, Kenya, South Africa and the United Arab Emirates. However, routes change regularly, so it is best to check before booking for the latest information regarding airlines visiting the archipelago.

Passport/Visa

Visitors to Seychelles receive a visa on arrival valid for up to one month. This can then be extended at no extra charge to up to three months from the date of arrival. When arriving at immigration you will usually need to show a valid return or onward ticket (if you do not have a ticket, you will be required to purchase one before being allowed to enter the country), proof of accommodation in Seychelles, and a passport that is valid for six months after your departure from Seychelles.

Before departing for Seychelles, it is important to check with your country of nationality to see if there is any additional information or permissions needed for you to be granted a Seychelles tourist visa.

ACCOMMODATION

There is a wide range of accommodation available in Seychelles, with something to suit most people's budgets in the mid and high-range. Self-catering flats and small guest houses offer a more affordable option and are plentiful on the islands of Mahé, Praslin and La Digue. These islands also boast a selection of mid-range and luxury resorts. At the higher end of the scale, certain islands offer a 'one island, one resort' package, 'for that exclusive island paradise experience'.

MONEY

The Seychelles rupee (SCR) is the currency of Seychelles. It is difficult to exchange outside Seychelles, so make sure not to withdraw too much. Although foreign currency is widely accepted in hotels and guest houses, Seychelles rupees are necessary for incidental purchases from markets or roadside stalls. Otherwise, it is possible to pay for purchases by card in most shops. For those wishing to obtain rupees, ATMs are common on the three main islands and accept most international debit cards. Alternatively, foreign currency such as US dollars (US$), pounds (GBP) and euros (€) can be exchanged at banks or a Bureau de Change. International bank branches that can be found in Seychelles are: ABSA, Mauritius Commercial Bank (MCB), Bank of Baroda and Nouvobanq. Euros are usually the preferred foreign currency, and you will sometimes find prices quoted in this tender.

TRANSPORT

There are various options available for getting around the islands, ranging from road transport to boats and aircraft.

Buses

The most affordable way to see the islands of Mahé and Praslin is by using the public bus service. The ubiquitous blue Tata buses, operated by the Seychelles Public Transport Company (SPTC), service most areas of the two islands and are well used by locals. Details of the bus schedule can be obtained at the central bus station in Victoria or on the SPTC website. Buses run regularly throughout the week during the day, with a decreased service on Sundays and public holidays, and little to no service after dark.

Taxis

Taxis are widely available on Mahé, Praslin and La Digue, and your hotel or guest house can arrange one for you. The majority of taxis are modern and clean, and while they are a convenient mode of transport, they are relatively expensive and are most useful in the evenings, when public transport is not available. Make sure you use a registered taxi and avoid pirate taxis, which are common, particularly at the ferry terminals.

Car Hire

In Seychelles, vehicles drive on the left-hand side of the road. The roads in Seychelles can be narrow, twisting and steep, but are in relatively good condition. Traffic in and around Victoria can sometimes be congested, particularly in the early mornings and late afternoons. If you plan to explore Mahé and Praslin, or are staying at accommodation a little out of the way, hiring a car is a good option for getting around.

There are numerous car-hire companies on Mahé and Praslin. Details of these companies can usually be obtained at your hotel or guest house, or from a phone directory. A variety of cars is available for hire, including automatic and manual models. You will need to show a valid driving licence in order to hire a car, and to provide details of a credit card.

Ferry

There is a reliable ferry service from Mahé to Praslin and La Digue, and from Praslin to La Digue. The Cat Cocos ferry is a modern catamaran and the journey takes around one hour from Mahé to Praslin, and an hour and 15 minutes from Mahé to La Digue. The ferry leaves from Inter Island Quay on Mahé, where there is also a Cat Cocos office. A smaller ferry service also operates from Praslin to La Digue.

Aircraft

Air Seychelles operates a domestic route between Mahé and Praslin, with several flights a day from the domestic terminal on Mahé. The flight takes about 15 minutes and provides the quickest way to travel between the two islands. The airline also flies to Bird Island and Denis, with the price of the flight built into the cost of the hotel package. Resorts on the outer islands are reached by planes operated by the Island Development Company (IDC), with flights leaving from the IDC airstrip.

ITINERARY

Most people visiting Seychelles base themselves on one of the three main islands, which are within easy reach of each other. For those spending two weeks in the archipelago, it is well worth spending at least a few days on each of the islands. Each has its own charm and attractions, and a vacation that takes in all three provides the opportunity to see much of Seychelles' endemic wildlife. Day trips to the seabird islands of Aride and Cousin are also recommended. If time allows, visits to coralline Bird Island, with its Sooty Tern colony (March–October) and nesting sea turtles (year-round, but primarily during November–January), are worthwhile.

The coralline islands that make up the outer islands group offer a different experience from that of the granitic islands. There are daily flights to Desroches Island, where it is possible to stay at the Four Seasons Resort. However, the island is dominated by coconut palms and, aside from nesting Wedge-tailed Shearwaters and sea turtles, offers little for those in search of terrestrial wildlife. Alphonse in the Amirantes group also has a resort and is a popular destination for fly fishing. Wildlife tours to the neighbouring St Francois atoll are regularly organized, taking in the tiny island of Bijoutier. St Francois hosts a small breeding colony of Red-footed Boobies, but also attracts very large numbers of roosting birds of this species that are of unknown origin (but currently under study). It is additionally possible to see frigatebirds in the coastal vegetation.

Accommodation is also available on the raised coralline islands of Astove and Cosmoledo, where the flora and fauna more closely resemble those of northern Madagascar than that of the Seychelles granitic islands. The terrestrial fauna of Cosmoledo is particularly rich.

GLOSSARY

abdomen Part of an insect or crustacean's body that contains the digestive organs. Located behind thorax.
annulus External circular ring commonly found in segmented animals.
antenna (pl. **antennae**) In animals, pair of long, thin sensory appendages located on heads of insects, crustaceans and some arthropods.
archipelago Group of islands or stretch of ocean containing a number of islands.
biodiversity The variety of plant and animal species found globally, or in a particular habitat or region.
calyx (of plants) Sepals of a flower, which typically form protective whorl around flower in bud.
carapace Hard upper shell of tortoise, turtle, crustacean or arachnid.
chrysalis Insect pupa of butterfly or moth and the name for hard outer layer of pupa.
dengue Tropical disease transmitted by mosquitos, resulting in fever and acute pains in the joints.
ecosystem Biological community of interacting organisms and their physical environment.
endemic Native or restricted to a certain area.
Exclusive Economic Zone (**EEZ**) Area of water and seabed within a certain distance of a country's coastline, to which the country claims exclusive rights for fishing, exploration and additional economic activities.
fauna Animal species of a particular, period, habitat or region.
flora Plant species of a particular period, habitat or region.
frond Leaf-like part of a fern or palm.
genus Group of organisms having common characteristics distinct from those of other such groupings. Taxonomic category that ranks above species and below family.
glacis Rocky hill or ridge that rises abruptly from the surrounding area. Also known as inselberg.
Gondwana Large continental area believed to have existed in the southern hemisphere and to have resulted from the break-up of the supercontinent of Pangea in Mesozoic times, 200 million years ago.
granitics Term used to describe the collection of Seychelles granitic islands.
inflorescence Arrangement of flowers on a plant, or entire flowerhead of plant, including stems, stalks and flowers.
intertidal zone Area of coast that is covered at high tide and exposed at low tide.
invasive species Non-native species that has been introduced deliberately or otherwise, and negatively alters its new environment.
invertebrate Any animal lacking a backbone or spinal cord.
IUCN Red List of Threatened Species International Union for Conservation of Nature's comprehensive inventory of the conservation status of global plant and animal species.

kernel (of plants) Soft and usually edible part of a nut or seed contained within its shell.
lanceolate (of leaves) Narrow and oval-shaped leaves tapering to a point at each end.
native (of animals or plants) Species indigenous to a place.
NGO Non-governmental organization.
nocturnal Occurring, or active, at night.
parthenogenetic Refers to development of an embryo from an unfertilized egg cell.
pinnate (of plants) Leaf with leaflets located on either side of stem, typically opposite each other and in pairs.
plastron (of animals) Underside of a tortoise or turtle shell. Ventral plate in certain invertebrate animals.
proboscis Nose of mammal or elongated sucking mouthpart in insect.
propagule (of mangroves) Seed of a mangrove, which germinates while still on the tree, before dispersing.
pupa Life stage of an insect transforming between an immature and a mature stage.
sp. (pl. **spp.**) Species.
tendril (of plants) Slender climbing appendage of a plant, which twines around suitable support.
terrestrial (of animals or plants) Living on land; not in water.
thorax Segments of an insect or crustacean's body located in front of abdomen.
translocation (of animals) Intentional capture and release of a species into the wild to establish or re-establish a population.
vagrant (of birds) Bird that has strayed from the usual range of its migratory route.

KEY TO ABBREVIATIONS IN SPECIES DESCRIPTIONS

e Endemic

n Native

r Resident

i Introduced

m Migrant

SEYCHELLES FAUNA

TERRESTRIAL MAMMALS

Due to their isolated location, the Seychelles islands lack native ground-dwelling terrestrial species, and are home to only five species of bat. By contrast, the waters of the nation's EEZ are home to a variety of whales and dolphins, and the Aldabra atoll to a small population of Dugongs.

Following human settlement, various mammals were introduced to the islands. These included dogs, cats, cattle, goats, pigs, rabbits, hares, tenrecs and rodents. The latter proved to be particularly destructive, impacting heavily on lizards, giant tortoises, invertebrates and seabird populations, as well as on plant communities. Successful rat eradications have been undertaken on certain islands with important seabird nesting populations.

Sheath-tailed Bat *Coleura seychellensis* WINGSPAN 25cm ⓔ

(Sousouri bannan)

INNER ISLANDS Mahé, Silhouette. **IUCN** Critically Endangered.

The Sheath-tailed Bat is so called due to the membrane that stretches between its hindlegs. A small bat with brown fur and a short tail, it roosts in granite caves by day and feeds on flying insects in the evening and at night. Females give birth to a single offspring. Less than 100 individuals are believed to remain across a handful of sites. This may be the most endangered species of bat in the world today.

Seychelles Fruit Bat *Pteropus seychellensis* WINGSPAN 110cm ⓔ

(Sousouri)

INNER ISLANDS Granitic islands. **IUCN** Least Concern.

The Seychelles Fruit Bat is a large bat weighing more than 500g. The dark wings and muzzle contrast with the yellow-orange head and upper body. The bats roost in groups during the day and can often be seen hanging upside down in trees. They are active in the early mornings and evenings, when they feed on nectar and fruits, with a preference for introduced fruit trees, including mango, bringing them into close proximity to human habitation. The bats can be very loud when feeding in groups, and the noise of squabbling fruit bats is a familiar sound on the larger inhabited islands. They are hunted in small numbers for human consumption.

Sheath-tailed Bat

Seychelles Fruit Bat

Aldabra Fruit Bat *Pteropus aldabrensis* **WINGSPAN** 100cm (e)

(Sousouri)

OUTER ISLANDS Aldabra atoll. **IUCN** Endangered.

Slightly smaller than the Seychelles Fruit Bat (p. 14), the Aldabra Fruit Bat has a paler head and neck. It feeds on a variety of fruits, including figs, and is often seen foraging in trees near the settlement on Picard Island. This species does not seem to form large gatherings in trees during the day. Recorded from all of Aldabra's main islands, there are believed to be fewer than 250 mature adults remaining, though the population is currently stable.

Brown Rat, Black Rat *Rattus norvegicus, R. rattus* (i)

(Lera)

INNER ISLANDS Most islands, exceptions being Aride, Bird, Cousin, Cousine, Denis, Frégate, North Island, Recifs. **OUTER ISLANDS** Most islands, exceptions being African Banks, D'Arros and St Joseph atoll, Desnoeufs, Marie-Louise, St Francois.
IUCN Least Concern.

Black Rats were probably introduced to Seychelles by traders as far back as the ninth century, while Brown Rats did not arrive until the second half of the twentieth century. Both the Brown Rat and Black Rat are common on the larger granitic islands, where they impact negatively on endemic fauna. On Mahé they are particularly abundant and are a nuisance around human habitation. The Brown Rat (pictured) is larger than the Black Rat and has a shorter tail. Both species are capable of climbing trees, though Black Rats are more proficient and will often spend time in the canopy of coconut trees.

Tenrec *Tenrec ecaudatus* **LENGTH** 35cm (i)

(Tang)

INNER ISLANDS Mahé, Praslin, Therèse. **IUCN** Least Concern.

The Tenrec has a light brown body covered in spines and lacking a tail, and a pale pink, elongated snout covered in large whiskers. Its powerful jaws enable it to feed on a variety of fruits, lizards and insects. It remains underground during the dry season, giving birth to young during the rainy north-west monsoon. There are several small young in a single litter, with distinctive pale stripes. Tenrecs are a food source in other parts of the Indian Ocean and were probably brought to Seychelles for that reason, but they are no longer consumed in Seychelles.

Aldabra Fruit Bat

Brown Rat

Tenrec

Tenrec juvenile

BIRDS

Although almost 300 bird species have been recorded within the Seychelles archipelago, most of the sightings represent occasional vagrants. However, about 30 breeding land-bird species are found on the granitic islands, 12 of which are endemic to Seychelles. Mahé provides an excellent opportunity for the bird enthusiast to encounter a number of endemic species, while several of the smaller cat- and rat-free islands have populations of translocated endemic birds.

While the majority of tourists remain in the granitic island group, visitors who venture to the coralline islands can encounter a variety of seabirds, including colonies of Red-footed Boobies on Aldabra, Cosmoledo, St Francois and Farquhar atolls, Sooty Terns on Bird Island, Cosmoledo atoll, and Wedge-tailed Shearwaters on Alphonse and Desroches Islands.

Sadly, a number of introduced bird species are also prevalent, several of which have become competitors of the native species. The Common Myna is one example that can be encountered on all of the larger granitic islands, where it competes with endemic birds and preys on native lizards.

Seychelles Kestrel *Falco araeus* LENGTH 23cm (e)

(Katiti Sesel)

INNER ISLANDS Mahé, Praslin, Silhouette, North Island. **IUCN** Vulnerable.

The smallest of the kestrel species, the Seychelles Kestrel has brown to red upperparts and a dark grey head. The underparts are beige to cream, while the tail is grey with black bars and the legs are bright yellow. The species feeds on insects, lizards and small birds, and is often seen perching on telegraph wires or the roofs of buildings. Breeding occurs predominantly during the north-west monsoon, with females laying two eggs.

Madagascar Kestrel *Falco newtoni* LENGTH 30cm (n)

(Katiti)

OUTER ISLANDS Aldabra atoll. **IUCN** Least Concern.

Larger than the Seychelles Kestrel (above), the Madagascar Kestrel has a restricted range and is found only in Madagascar and on Aldabra atoll. It has a white underside with black spots, and a brown back and crown. It feeds on small lizards and invertebrates.

Amur Falcon *Falco amurensis* LENGTH 23cm (m)

INNER & OUTER ISLANDS Granitic islands, Amirantes group south to Alphonse. **IUCN** Least Concern.

The male Amur Falcon has a predominantly grey body, and the female a spotted white breast. The legs, bill-base and eye-ring are orange. The species is a regular annual visitor to Seychelles as it crosses the Indian Ocean from north-east Asia on its way to east Africa.

Seychelles Kestrel

Madagascar Kestrel

Amur Falcon

Barn Owl *Tyto alba* **LENGTH** 35cm i

(Ibou)

INNER ISLANDS Most granitic islands. **IUCN** Least Concern.

The Barn Owl was introduced to Seychelles in an attempt to control rats. However, it has had little effect on the rat population and instead became a major predator of native bird species. A large owl with a pale head and underparts, it roosts by day and is active at night. It produces a distinctive shrieking call, which can often be heard near human habitation.

Seychelles Scops Owl *Otus insularis* **LENGTH** 23cm e

(Syer)

INNER ISLANDS Mahé. **IUCN** Endangered.

The Seychelles Scops Owl is a small, grey to brown owl with dark, mottled plumage, and has a distinctive call, said to resemble the noise of a saw. Rarely seen, it is only found on Mahé, where it is confined to mid- and high-altitude forests. It feeds on invertebrates and lizards.

Madagascar Nightjar *Caprimulgus madagascariensis* **LENGTH** 40cm n

(Sonmey)

OUTER ISLANDS Aldabra atoll. **IUCN** Least Concern.

Only found on Aldabra atoll and in Madagascar, this nightjar's mottled grey-brown body and series of whiskers on the head provide excellent camouflage. During the day it remains on the ground, where it is difficult to see among the leaf litter. It feeds at night, catching insects in flight.

Aldabra White-throated Rail *Dryolimnas cuvieri aldabranus* **LENGTH** 30cm e

(Tyomityo)

OUTER ISLANDS Aldabra atoll. **IUCN** Least Concern.

While this species is listed on the IUCN Red List as being of Least Concern, the subspecies found on only three islands of the Aldabra atoll is believed to be the last flightless bird in the Indian Ocean. It once occurred on all the islands of Aldabra, as well as on Assumption, Cosmoledo and Astove atolls, but was eradicated in many cases by feral cats. This small, ground-dwelling bird has a chestnut body, with a white throat-patch and a formidable beak used for catching insects. It makes distinctive loud vocalizations.

Barn Owl

Seychelles Scops Owl

Madagascar Nightjar

Aldabra White-throated Rail

Seychelles Blue Pigeon *Alectroenas pulcherrimus* LENGTH 25cm e

(Pizon olande)

INNER ISLANDS Granitic islands, Bird, Denis. **IUCN** Least Concern.
This unmistakable pigeon has a dark blue body, light grey head, neck and breast, yellow bill, red wattle around the eyes and red crest. It was hunted in the past, but the population increased once the practice died out. It feeds on fruits and seeds, and is often seen in and around gardens.

Comoros Blue Pigeon *Alectroenas sganzini* LENGTH 25cm n

(Pizon olande Aldabra)

OUTER ISLANDS Aldabra atoll. **IUCN** Near Threatened.
The Comoros Blue Pigeon is restricted to Aldabra atoll and the Comoros. It has dark blue wings, underside and tail, a white head, neck and breast, and a distinctive red eye-ring. It feeds on small fruits and can often be seen perched high in trees during the day. It often flies between the different islands of Aldabra atoll.

Barred Ground Dove *Geopelia striata* LENGTH 23cm i

(Tourtrel koko)

INNER ISLANDS Granitic islands, Bird, Denis. **OUTER ISLANDS** Coëtivy, D'Arros, St Joseph, Desroches, Farquhar atoll. **IUCN** Least Concern.
The Barred Ground Dove is a small grey dove with narrow dark bars and a long tail. The breast is often pinkish and the bill and eye-ring are pale blue. It is common throughout the granitic islands, where it can easily be seen in gardens and urban areas. It has a very distinctive cooing call.

Feral pigeon *Columba livia* LENGTH 35cm i

(Pizon domestik)

INNER ISLANDS La Digue, Mahé, Praslin, Silhouette. **IUCN** Least Concern.
Believed to have been introduced to Seychelles midway through the twentieth century, feral pigeons have variable colouration, most often dark grey, but also black and white. They are common in urban areas, particularly in Victoria and Perseverance on Mahé.

Madagascar Turtle Dove *Nesoenas picturatus* LENGTH 35cm n

(Tourtrel dezil)

INNER ISLANDS Granitic islands. **OUTER ISLANDS** Aldabra atoll, Amirantes group, Cosmoledo atoll, Desroches. **IUCN** Least Concern.
A large purple to brown pigeon, the Madagascar Turtle Dove is common in woodland and gardens on the granitic islands. This species has a complex taxonomy and is thought to be made up of different subspecies, including endemic and introduced races. Outside of Aldabra, it is unlikely that many pure forms remain.

Seychelles Blue Pigeon

Comoros Blue Pigeon

Barred Ground Dove

Feral pigeon

Madagascar Turtle Dove

Seychelles Black Parrot *Coracopsis barklyi* LENGTH 30cm e

(Kato nwar)

INNER ISLANDS Breeds on Praslin. **IUCN** Vulnerable.

This dark brown parrot with dark legs and beak is endemic to Seychelles, where it is restricted to the island of Praslin and thought to visit Curieuse. It feeds on the fruits of introduced and endemic palms and trees. The Vallée de Mai offers the best opportunity to see the bird.

Madagascar Coucal *Centropus toulou* LENGTH 45cm n

(Toulouz)

OUTER ISLANDS Aldabra atoll. **IUCN** Least Concern.

The Madagascar Coucal was formerly found on Assumption and Cosmoledo in Seychelles, but is now restricted to Aldabra atoll. A large bird with a black body and chestnut-coloured wings, it feeds on insects and lizards, often pulling back the bark of Casuarina trees to reach them.

Seychelles Bulbul *Hypsipetes crassirostris* LENGTH 25cm e

(Merl)

INNER ISLANDS La Digue, Mahé, Praslin, Silhouette. **IUCN** Least Concern.

The Seychelles Bulbul is a dark brown bird with a black crest and bright orange bill and legs. Juveniles have brown beaks and legs. It is a commonly seen species on the larger granitic islands, where its loud, squawking calls can be heard in gardens and forests. It is a charismatic species that will often approach humans closely.

Seychelles Magpie Robin *Copsychus sechellarum* LENGTH 24cm e

(Pi santez)

INNER ISLANDS Aride, Cousin, Cousine, Denis, Frégate. **IUCN** Endangered.

The Seychelles Magpie Robin is a distinctive black-and-white bird with a wingspan of about 30cm. It prefers lowland forests, where it feeds on insects in the leaf litter. The species had declined to 12 individuals on Frégate Island in the 1960s, before intensive conservation measures, including translocations to other islands, helped the population to increase to almost 300 individuals. It is particularly susceptible to predation by feral cats.

Seychelles Black Parrot

Madagascar Coucal

Seychelles Bulbul

Seychelles Magpie Robin

Seychelles Black Paradise Flycatcher *Terpsiphone corvina*

LENGTH 20cm (37cm with tail streamers) e
(Vev)

INNER ISLANDS Curieuse, Denis, La Digue. **IUCN** Vulnerable.
The males of this endemic flycatcher are black with long tail streamers and bright blue eyes and beak. The females have a chestnut plumage with a white belly and black head. A forest-dwelling species, breeding occurs all year round and the small, cup-shaped nests can be found in the lower branches of trees. It feeds on insects and spiders. A number of the flycatchers have been translocated from La Digue to Curieuse and Denis Islands.

Seychelles Warbler *Acrocephalus sechellensis* **LENGTH** 13cm e

(Timerl dezil)

INNER ISLANDS Aride, Cousin, Cousine, Denis Frégate. **IUCN** Near Threatened.
This small, olive-brown to grey bird with mustard underparts and a slender bill favours Pisonia forest and dense shrubland, where it feeds on insects. Its population was down to less than 30 birds on Cousin Island in the 1960s, but translocations to other islands have seen an increase in numbers.

Seychelles White-eye *Zosterops modestus* **LENGTH** 10cm e

(Zwazo linet Sesel)

INNER ISLANDS Conception, Cousine, Frégate, North Island, Mahé. **IUCN** Vulnerable.
The Seychelles White-eye is a small, grey to brown bird with a characteristic white eye-ring. The underparts of its body often have a yellow tinge. The species was introduced to Cousine, Frégate and North Islands as a conservation measure. It is restricted to a few locations on Mahé.

Madagascar White-eye *Zosterops maderaspatanus* **LENGTH** 10cm n

(Zwazo linet Malgas)

OUTER ISLANDS Aldabra atoll, Astove, Cosmoledo atoll. **IUCN** Least Concern.
This white-eye species is found on a number of western Indian Ocean islands, with two subspecies identified in Seychelles. It has olive-green wings and tail, a yellow throat and grey belly, and an incomplete white eye-ring with a gap in front of the eye. It feeds in the open during the day, favouring insects, fruits and flower buds.

Aldabra Drongo *Dicrurus aldabranus* **LENGTH** 25cm e

(Moulanba)

OUTER ISLANDS Aldabra atoll. **IUCN** Near Threatened.
The Aldabra Drongo is a medium-sized black bird with a deeply forked tail. It feeds on a variety of insects caught on the wing. Endemic to Aldabra atoll, the population is believed to be stable at approximately 1,000 birds. A gregarious species, it is often observed chasing off larger birds.

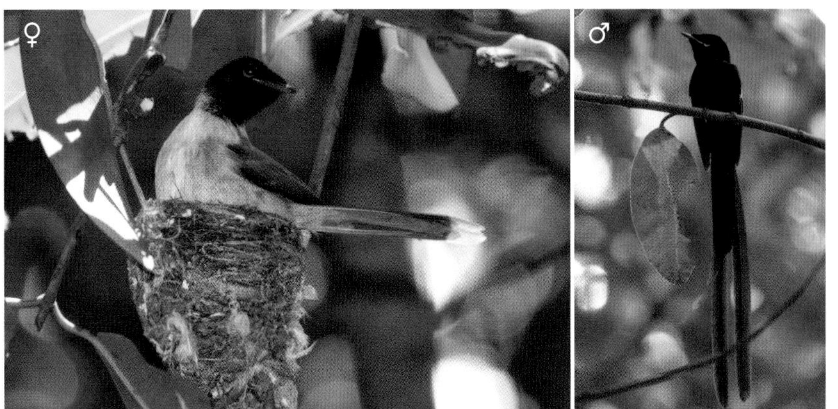

Seychelles Black Paradise Flycatcher

Seychelles Warbler

Seychelles White-eye

Madagascar White-eye

Aldabra Drongo

Seychelles Sunbird *Cinnyris dussumieri* **LENGTH** 11cm e

(Kolibri)

INNER ISLANDS Most islands. **IUCN** Least Concern.

A small grey to brown bird with a long, curved bill, the male Seychelles Sunbird has a metallic blue chest and a small tuft of bright orange below the wings. The species is found in a range of habitats and is a common sight in most gardens. It has been introduced to Bird Island.

Souimanga Sunbird *Cinnyris sovimanga* **LENGTH** 10cm n

(Kolibri Aldabra)

OUTER ISLANDS Aldabra atoll. **IUCN** Least Concern.

The Souimanga Sunbird is found in Madagascar and on Aldabra atoll, where there is an endemic race (*C. s. aldabrensis*). Males have a metallic blue-green head, pale yellow belly and brown wings. Females have grey-brown upperparts and a pale yellow belly.

Common Myna *Acridotheres tristis* **LENGTH** 23cm i

(Marten)

INNER ISLANDS Granitic islands. **IUCN** Least Concern.

The Common Myna has a dark body, becoming black on the neck and head. The eye-ring, bill and legs are yellow. The species is very common on many of the granitic islands, where it often harasses native wildlife. Eradication programmes have been attempted on several of the inner islands.

Madagascar Fody *Foudia madagascariensis* **LENGTH** 13cm i

(Sren)

INNER ISLANDS Granitic islands, Bird, Denis. **OUTER ISLANDS** Assumption, D'Arros, Denis, Desroches, Farquhar atoll, Platte, Remire, St Joseph atoll, St Pierre.
IUCN Least Concern.

Breeding male Madagascar Fodys are a distinctive orange-red colour with brown wings and tail. Females and non-breeding males are a pale brown colour. The species is common in gardens and urban areas, and often congregates near hotel restaurants in search of food.

Seychelles Fody *Foudia sechellarum* **LENGTH** 13cm e

(Toktok)

INNER ISLANDS Aride, Cousin, Cousine, Denis, Frégate. **OUTER ISLANDS** D'Arros.
IUCN Near Threatened.

This species resembles the female Madagascar Fody (above), with a brown body and darker streaks on the wings. Males have yellow plumage around the bill when breeding. The birds feed on a variety of fruits and insects.

Seychelles Sunbird

Souimanga Sunbird

Common Myna

Madagascar Fody

Seychelles Fody

Aldabra Fody *Foudia aldabrana* **LENGTH** 13cm e

(Sren Aldabra)

OUTER ISLANDS Aldabra atoll. **IUCN** Endangered.

Found only on Aldabra atoll, the male Aldabra Fody has a red head and yellow belly, while the female is brown. The birds feeds on seeds and build a hanging woven nest made of twigs and grasses.

Common Waxbill *Estrilda astrild* **LENGTH** 13cm i

(Bengali)

INNER ISLANDS La Digue, Mahé. **OUTER ISLANDS** Alphonse. **IUCN** Least Concern.

This small brown finch has pinkish-white underparts and a bright orange-red bill and eye-stripe. It is restricted to areas of scrub and grassland, where it can be seen in small flocks. It feeds predominantly on grass seeds, but also on small invertebrates.

Seychelles Swiftlet *Aerodramus elaphrus* **LENGTH** 11cm e

(Irondel Sesel)

INNER ISLANDS La Digue, Mahé, Praslin. **IUCN** Vulnerable.

A small grey to brown bird with a forked tail, the Seychelles Swiftlet is commonly seen feeding on the wing during the early mornings and evenings. It builds nests made of plant material and saliva in caves.

Wedge-tailed Shearwater *Puffinus pacificus* **LENGTH** 45cm n

(Fouke)

INNER ISLANDS Breeds at Aride, Bird, Cousin, Cousine, Mamelles, North Island, Recif, St Anne. **OUTER ISLANDS** Breeds at Alphonse, D'Arros, Desnoeufs, Desroches, Marie-Louise, St Joseph atoll. **IUCN** Least Concern.

A dark brown bird with a wedge-shaped tail, this shearwater feeds on fish, squid and crustaceans. During the breeding season adults spend most of the day at sea, returning to the colony after dark. They make a distinctive ghostly wailing sound.

Tropical Shearwater *Puffinus bailloni* **LENGTH** 33cm n

(Riga)

INNER ISLANDS Breeds at Aride, Cousin, Cousine, Recif. **OUTER ISLANDS** Breeds at Aldabra atoll, Desnoeufs, Desroches. **IUCN** Least Concern.

This relatively small shearwater has a dark head and back, and white on the underside. It nests in burrows on rat-free islands, and feeds on fish and squid caught at sea. As in the case of the Wedge-tailed Shearwater (above), poaching has depleted populations on unprotected islands.

Aldabra Fody

Common Waxbill

Seychelles Swiftlet

Wedge-tailed Shearwater

Tropical Shearwater

White-tailed Tropicbird *Phaethon lepturus* **LENGTH** 80cm ⓝ

(Payanke lake blan)

INNER ISLANDS Breeds on granitic islands, Bird, Denis. **OUTER ISLANDS** Aldabra atoll, Amirantes, Cosmoledo atoll. **IUCN** Least Concern.

The White-tailed Tropicbird is a large white bird with black wing-tips and a black bar through the eye. It has yellow legs and bill, and long white tail streamers. A solitary breeder preferring to nest on the ground, it builds nests in trees or on ledges on islands with predators. White-tailed Tropicbirds are one of the most commonly observed seabirds flying high above the larger granitic islands.

Red-tailed Tropicbird *Phaethon rubricauda* **LENGTH** 80cm ⓝ

(Payanke lake rouz)

INNER ISLANDS Breeds at Aride. **OUTER ISLANDS** Breeds at Aldabra atoll, Cosmoledo atoll. **IUCN** Least Concern.

A large white bird with broad wings, red beak and narrow red tail, the Red-tailed Tropicbird is common within the Aldabra group, but rare on the granitic islands, with only a few breeding pairs on Aride. It feeds on fish, squid and crustaceans.

Lesser Frigatebird *Fregata ariel* **LENGTH** 80cm ⓝ

(Pti fregat)

OUTER ISLANDS Breeds at Aldabra atoll. **IUCN** Least Concern.

The Lesser Frigatebird is a large seabird with a dark body and narrow spurs of white on the undersides of the wings. Females and immature birds also have a white breast. Males have an inflatable throat-patch that is used in sexual displays.

Great Frigatebird *Fregata minor* **LENGTH** 105cm ⓝ

(Gran fregat)

OUTER ISLANDS Breeds at Aldabra, Cosmoledo. **IUCN** Least Concern.

Males are mainly black with a red throat patch during the breeding season. Females have a white throat and breast. Both sexes lack the white wing-spurs found on the underside of the Lesser Fregatebird (above). Located in the top of mangroves, the nests are built out of small tree branches and the female will lay a single egg, which once hatched, will take up to six months to fledge. Great Frigatebids feed on squid and fish, often stealing the prey of other seabirds.

White-tailed Tropicbird

Red-tailed Tropicbird

Lesser Frigatebird

Great Frigatebird

Brown Booby *Sula leucogaster* **LENGTH** 74cm n

(Fou kapisen)

OUTER ISLANDS Breeds at Boudeuse, Cosmoledo atoll. **IUCN** Least Concern.
A large seabird, the Brown Booby is predominantly brown with a white breast and centre of underwings. Breeding males have a blue eye-ring, while females have a yellow eye-ring. This is the rarest booby species to be found in Seychelles.

Red-footed Booby *Sula sula* **LENGTH** 75cm n

(Fou bet)

OUTER ISLANDS Breeds at Aldabra atoll, Cosmoledo atoll, Farquhar atoll, Marie-Louise, St Francois. **IUCN** Least Concern.
The Red-footed Booby is a large seabird with a white body and dark trailing edge to the wing. It has distinctive red legs and feet and a pale blue bill. Juveniles are dark grey to brown. Adult brown morphs also occur. It feeds on fish and squid.

Great Crested Tern *Thalasseus bergii* **LENGTH** 49cm n

(Golan sardin)

OUTER ISLANDS Breeds at African Banks, Aldabra atoll, Etoile. **IUCN** Least Concern.
This large tern has a white body and grey upperparts, black legs and a black cap. The yellow bill becomes duller outside the breeding season. The species is commonly seen along the coast of Mahé, where it feeds on fish and squid.

Roseate Tern *Sterna dougallii* **LENGTH** 38cm n

(Dyanman roz)

INNER ISLANDS Breeds at Aride. **OUTER ISLANDS** Breeds at African Banks, Etoile, Farquhar, St Joseph atoll. **IUCN** Least Concern.
This medium-sized tern has grey upperparts and white underparts, a forked white tail, red legs, a black cap and a red bill, which becomes duller outside the breeding season. It feeds on small fish.

Black-naped Tern *Sterna sumatrana* **LENGTH** 30cm n

(Dyanman likou nwanr)

OUTER ISLANDS Breeds at African Banks, Aldabra atoll, Cosmoledo atoll, Farquhar atoll, St Francois, St Joseph atoll. **IUCN** Least Concern.
Pale grey above and white below, with black legs and a black bill, this small tern also has a distinctive black band running from eye to eye. It feeds on small fish and marine invertebrates, and is a vagrant to the granitic islands.

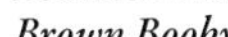

Brown Booby

Red-footed Booby

Great Crested Tern

Roseate Tern

Black-naped Tern

Bridled Tern *Onychoprion anaethetus* **LENGTH** 35cm n

(Fansen)

INNER ISLANDS Breeds at Aride, Booby Island, Cousin, Cousine, L'Ilot Frégate, Récif. **OUTER ISLANDS** Breeds at Cosmoledo atoll, Desneoufs. **IUCN** Least Concern.
This medium-sized tern has grey to brown upperparts and white underparts, a black bill and black legs. It is similar in appearance to the Sooty Tern (below), although in the Bridled Tern a white streak extends behind the eye. It feeds on fish and squid.

Sooty Tern *Onychoprion fuscatus* **LENGTH** 39cm n

(Golet)

INNER ISLANDS Breeds at Aride, Bird, Cousine, L'Ilot Frégate, Récif.
OUTER ISLANDS Breeds at African Banks, Cosmoledo atoll, Deneoufs, Etoile.
IUCN Least Concern.
Similar in appearance to the Bridled Tern (above), in the Sooty Tern the white streak on the forehead does not extend behind the eye. The most frequently ringed bird in Seychelles, this species is known to make some incredible journeys across the Indian Ocean.

Brown Noddy *Anous stolidus* **LENGTH** 40cm n

(Makwa)

INNER & OUTER ISLANDS Breeds at most rat-free islands. **IUCN** Least Concern.
Noddies get their common name from their courtship display, in which they nod to each other. The Brown Noddy is a dark brown tern with a grey cap and a sturdy black beak. A common seabird, it nests in palms and on the ground, and feeds on fish and squid.

Lesser Noddy *Anous tenuirostris* **LENGTH** 34cm n

(Kordonnyen)

INNER ISLANDS Breeds on Aride, Bird, Cousin, Cousine, Denis, Frégate.
OUTER ISLANDS Breeds on Marie-Louise, Rémire. **IUCN** Least Concern.
Similar in appearance to the Brown Noddy (above), the Lesser Noddy has a lighter build and a more slender beak. It is believed that Seychelles holds a significant amount of the world's Lesser Noddy population, with large colonies on Aride, Cousin and Cousine.

Fairy Tern *Gygis alba* **LENGTH** 33cm n

(Golan blan)

INNER ISLANDS Breeds on most granitic islands, Bird, Denis.
OUTER ISLANDS Breeds at Aldabra atoll, Alphonse atoll, Assumption, Cosmoledo atoll, Farquhar atoll. **IUCN** Least Concern.
The Fairy Tern is a completely white tern with bluish-black legs and bill. It lays a single egg directly on to the branches of trees, managing to breed successfully on islands with predators, and can even be seen in trees in central Victoria.

Bridled Tern

Sooty Tern

Brown Noddy

Lesser Noddy

Fairy Tern

Cattle Egret *Bubulcus ibis* **LENGTH** 55cm n

(Madanm paton)

INNER & OUTER ISLANDS Breeds on most islands. **IUCN** Least Concern.
A white egret with a yellow bill and black legs, the Cattle Egret's breeding plumage includes a golden crown, breast and back. It forms large colonies in trees and feeds on a variety of prey, including molluscs, fish, lizards and insects. It also scavengers and is present in large numbers near landfill sites.

Dimorphic Egret *Egretta gularis* **LENGTH** 55cm n

(Zegret blan e nwanr)

OUTER ISLANDS Aldabra atoll, Astove, Cosmoledo atoll. **IUCN** Not Evaluated.
The Dimorphic Egret occurs in two colour morphs, the more common white morph and the rarer dark grey morph, which has a white throat. It feeds on fish and crustaceans, and is frequently seen at the water's edge. The birds nests in low shrubs, often in large groups.

Grey Heron *Ardea cinerea* **LENGTH** 100cm n

(Floranten sann)

INNER & OUTER ISLANDS Most islands. **IUCN** Least Concern.
A large grey bird, paler below and with a black cap on the head, the Grey Heron's yellow bill and dull legs turn reddish during the breeding season. It is a common sight on many of the islands, including in Victoria, where it fishes along streams. It was previously exploited, but numbers are now increasing on the inner islands.

Striated Heron *Butorides striata* **LENGTH** 48cm n

(Manik ledo)

INNER & OUTER ISLANDS Most islands. **IUCN** Least Concern.
This small heron is green-grey on the back and wings, with light grey underparts. The legs and bill-base are yellow. It is common on most islands, where it can be seen fishing along shorelines and in coastal shallows.

Black-crowned Night Heron *Nycticorax nycticorax* **LENGTH** 65cm n

(Manik lannwit)

INNER ISLANDS Cousin, La Digue, Mahé, Praslin, Silhouette. **OUTER ISLANDS** St Joseph. **IUCN** Least Concern.
The Black-crowned Night Heron has a black back and crown with grey underparts, a distinctive red eye and a blue-black bill. It prefers wetlands, where it hunts at dusk and dawn. A recent colonizer to the inner granitic islands, it first bred there in the mid-1990s.

Cattle Egret

Dimorphic Egret

Grey Heron

Striated Heron

Black-crowned Night Heron

Common Moorhen *Gallinula chloropus* **LENGTH** 35cm n

(Pouldo)

INNER ISLANDS Bird, Denis and larger granitic islands. **IUCN** Least Concern.
A common wetland bird, the Common Moorhen has a dark brown to black body, a white line on the flanks, a bright red bill with a yellow tip, and yellow legs with large feet. It feeds on worms, snails, seeds and vegetation.

Madagascar Sacred Ibis *Threskiornis bernieri* **LENGTH** 80cm e

(Ibis Malgas)

OUTER ISLANDS Aldabra atoll. **IUCN** Endangered.
A large, ground-dwelling bird with white plumage, this endemic subspecies has black ornamental plumes on the back and a black head and neck. The iris is pale blue in colour. The birds feed on a variety of prey, including crabs, snails and small vertebrates.

Crab Plover *Dromas ardeola* **LENGTH** 35cm m

(Kavalye)

INNER & OUTER ISLANDS Encountered throughout Seychelles. **IUCN** Least Concern.
This black-and-white wading bird has a distinctive heavy bill and long, blue-grey legs. It feeds in lagoons and on mud flats, where it hunts for crabs. It can be seen in large flocks in the outer islands, and usually in small numbers in the granitic islands.

Pacific Golden Plover *Pluvialis fulva* **LENGTH** 25cm m

(Plovye dore)

INNER & OUTER ISLANDS Inner islands and Amirantes. **IUCN** Least Concern.
This slender plover has long legs and golden-yellow upperparts, becoming paler underneath. It is slightly smaller than the Grey Plover (below), which is duller in colour, and occurs in small numbers between October and April.

Grey Plover *Pluvialis squatarola* **LENGTH** 30cm m

(Plovye sann)

INNER & OUTER ISLANDS Throughout Seychelles. **IUCN** Least Concern.
A common plover with mottled grey plumage, the Grey Plover is present year-round and can often be seen solitarily or in small groups feeding along coastlines and mudflats. It feeds on crustaceans and molluscs.

Common Moorhen

Madagascar Sacred Ibis

Crab Plover

Pacific Golden Plover

Grey Plover

Sanderling *Calidris alba* **LENGTH** 20cm (m)

(Bekaso blan)

INNER & OUTER ISLANDS Throughout Seychelles. **IUCN** Least Concern.

A small wader, the Sanderling is silver to grey above with white underparts. The bill and legs are both black. It feeds along the shorelines of beaches, where it searches for worms, molluscs and crustaceans buried in the sand.

Whimbrel *Numenius phaeopus* **LENGTH** 40–46cm (m)

(Korbizo)

INNER & OUTER ISLANDS Throughout Seychelles. **IUCN** Least Concern.

A common wader on most islands with a mottled brown body and a distinctive brown eye-stripe, the Whimbrel's long, downwards curved bill is used for probing sand and mud for molluscs and crabs. The species has a loud, distinctive call, which it makes if approached too closely. Sometimes confused with the Eurasian Curlew, however, the Whimbrel is small with a shorter beak.

Common Greenshank *Tringa nebularia* **LENGTH** 34cm (m)

(Gran lapat ver)

INNER & OUTER ISLANDS Throughout Seychelles. **IUCN** Least Concern.

The Common Greenshank is an annual migrant with grey wings and back, white underparts, greenish-grey legs and a long, upturned bill. It feeds by moving its head from side to side in search of crustaceans and small fish. One of the most frequently sighted waders, particularly between November and April.

Ruddy Turnstone *Arenaria interpres* **LENGTH** 25cm (m)

(Sifler trakase)

INNER & OUTER ISLANDS Throughout Seychelles. **IUCN** Least Concern.

This short wader is probably the most common of the waders found in fish. One of the most frequently sighted waders, particularly between November and April. It is mainly brown above with white underparts. The legs are orange and the bill is black. It is found in small groups along sandy and rocky shorelines. It has a varied diet, which includes crustaceans, molluscs, insects and small fishes. A relatively long-lived wader, with an average lifespan of nearly ten years.

Sanderling

Whimbrel

Common Greenshank

Ruddy Turnstone

REPTILES

The reptiles of Seychelles consist of almost 30 species, 70 per cent of which are endemic. The geckos and skinks are particularly common around human habitation and are easily encountered on most of the islands. On Mahé, the Botanical Gardens have an enclosure with a small population of giant tortoises, which can also be seen at several of the hotels. The hiking trails on the larger granitic islands provide an opportunity to see snakes, while the Vallée de Mai on Praslin is home to chameleons and the Giant Bronze Gecko. Both Green and Hawksbill Turtles nest on Seychelles beaches, although Green Turtles are more common on the outer islands, and numbers of Hawksbill Turtles are decreasing on the three main populated islands.

Aldabra Giant Tortoise *Aldabrachelys gigantea* LENGTH 100cm e

(Torti ter)

INNER & OUTER ISLANDS Aldabra atoll hosts the only natural population; all other islands are now populated by animals derived from the Aldabra ancestral stock.
IUCN Vulnerable.
Several species of giant tortoise inhabited islands in the Indian Ocean, but they were heavily exploited with the arrival of humans. The only remaining natural population in the entire western Indian Ocean is that found at Aldabra atoll, where there are more than 100,000 tortoises. Giant tortoises from the Aldabra stock have been translocated to most of the islands of Seychelles, where they breed well, and they are also widespread in captivity throughout Seychelles. Giant tortoises did not originally occur in the Amirantes group when humans first arrived in Seychelles. The stock of giant tortoises that was certainly present in the inner islands of Seychelles at the time of human arrival was exterminated by a combination of human over-exploitation and predation by feral animals introduced by people (pigs, dogs, cats, rats and others). It is unclear whether the inner island tortoises were a separate species from those that now inhabit Aldabra atoll. Tortoises feed mainly on vegetation and can live for more than 150 years. They float well and are able to travel long distances between islands in that manner.

Aldabra Giant Tortoise

Seychelles Black Mud Terrapin *Pelusios subniger parietalis*

LENGTH 20cm ⓔ

(Torti Soupap)

INNER ISLANDS Cerf, Cousin, Frégate, La Digue, Mahé, North Island, Praslin, Silhouette, Ste Anne. **IUCN** Critically Endangered.

This terrapin has a dark grey carapace and a yellow to grey plastron with black patches. It is believed to be a subspecies of the mud terrapin native to eastern Africa. It is found in freshwater marshes, where it feeds on invertebrates, fish and fruits.

Seychelles Yellow-bellied Mud Turtle

Pelusios castanoides intergularis **LENGTH** 23cm ⓔ

(Torti Soupap)

INNER ISLANDS Cerf, Curieuse, Frégate, La Digue, Mahé, Praslin, Silhouette, Ste Anne. **IUCN** Critically Endangered.

This subspecies has a variable carapace colour ranging from dark brown to yellow. The plastron is yellow, the neck and limbs yellow-brown. It is found in wetlands, where it feeds on insects, fish and fruits. It buries itself in damp mud when its marshes dry out.

Green Turtle *Chelonia mydas* **LENGTH** Adults to 130cm (carapace length) ⓝ

(Torti)

INNER & OUTER ISLANDS Breeds on most islands in Seychelles, although it is most common in the remote southern islands of Aldabra atoll, Assumption, Cosmoledo atoll, and Farquhar atoll of the outer islands. **IUCN** Endangered.

Green Turtles are olive to brown in colour, and are named after the colour of their green fat. They breed at night. In the inner islands their nesting numbers are now very low, probably in response to over-exploitation by people. They are slightly more abundant in the outer coralline islands, and most abundant in the remote southern atolls. In Seychelles, adults feed primarily on seagrass. Although sea turtles are protected in Seychelles, some poaching for turtle meat still occurs.

Hawksbill Turtle *Eretmochelys imbricata*

LENGTH Adults to 95cm (carapace length) ⓝ

(Kare)

INNER & OUTER ISLANDS Breeds on most islands in Seychelles, although it is by far the most common in the inner islands and in the Amirantes island group. Breeds only in small numbers in the remote southern atolls where Green Turtles (above) are most abundant. **IUCN** Critically Endangered.

Hawksbill Turtles have a yellow to brown carapace and a distinctive hawk-like beak. The nesting season in Seychelles runs from September through to March, when females come ashore during daylight hours to nest. The eggs hatch after two months.

Seychelles Black Mud Terrapin

Seychelles Yellow-bellied Mud Turtle

Green Turtle

Hawksbill Turtle

Day Gecko *Phelsuma astriata* LENGTH 12cm e

(Lezar ver)

INNER ISLANDS Bird, Denis and granitic islands. **OUTER ISLANDS** Aldabra atoll, Amirantes, Astove. **IUCN** Least Concern.

The Day Gecko is a small, common gecko with a white belly and bright green body. It has irregular red markings on the dorsal side, often with a chevron between the eyes. The species has the ability to change colour intensity, depending on available light. It is found in a variety of habitats, including gardens, where it is often associated with native and introduced palms. It often enters buildings and can easily be observed during the day. It feeds on a variety of insects as well as smaller geckos.

Sundberg's Day Gecko *Phelsuma sundbergi* LENGTH 19cm e

(Lezar ver)

INNER ISLANDS Denis and all granitic islands. **OUTER ISLANDS** Amirantes, Astove, Cosmoledo atoll, Platte. **IUCN** Least Concern.

Sundberg's Day Gecko is the largest of the day gecko species found in Seychelles. Its body is predominantly green in colour, with some individuals displaying red spots on the dorsal surface. The eye-ring is yellow. The species is found in palm forests and Coconut plantations, as well as close to human habitation, where it will opportunistically consume uneaten food.

Gold Dust Day Gecko *Phelsuma laticauda* LENGTH 15cm r

(Lezar ver)

OUTER ISLANDS Farquhar atoll. **IUCN** Least Concern.

Native to Comoros and northern Madagascar, the Gold Dust Day Gecko is also found on Farquhar, although its origins are unclear. It has a green to yellow body with yellow dots on the neck and body, and blue eyelids. Three parallel red marks run along the lower back. It feeds on small insects and flower nectar.

Abbot's Day Gecko *Phelsuma abbotti* LENGTH 15cm n

(Lezar ver)

OUTER ISLANDS Aldabra atoll, Assumption. **IUCN** Least Concern.

A dark grey to green day gecko with a light-coloured eye-ring and belly, Abbot's Day Gecko occurs on palms and Casuarina trees, where it hides amongst the bark. It is preyed upon by bird species including the Madagascar Coucal. On Aldabra it is found in association with giant tortoises, where it is often seen on a tortoise's body.

Day Gecko

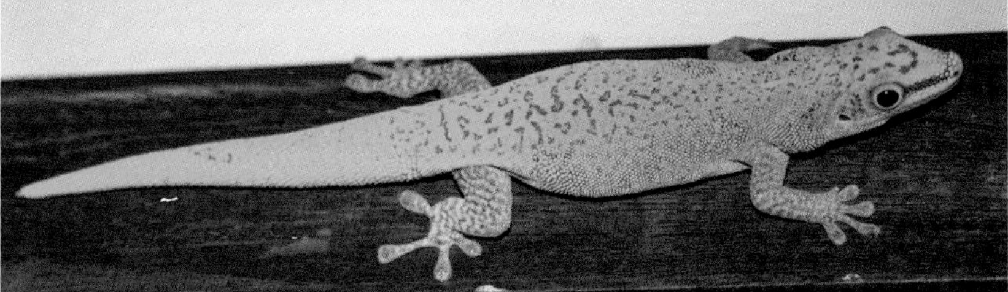

Sundberg's Day Gecko

Gold Dust Day Gecko

Abbot's Day Gecko

Stump-toed Gecko *Gehyra mutilata* **LENGTH** 10cm

(Lezar disik)

INNER & OUTER ISLANDS Most islands. **IUCN** Least Concern.

The Stump-toed Gecko has a pale grey to brown upper body that is either uniform or spotted. It is completely white underneath and has a flattened tail. A nocturnal lizard, it feeds on a variety of insects, as well as on smaller geckos of its own species. It is very common in human habitation, where it congregates near lights in search of a meal. It makes a characteristic 'tock' sound, which it repeats multiple times.

Asian House Gecko *Hemidactylus frenatus* **LENGTH** 13cm

(Lezar disik)

INNER & OUTER ISLANDS Most coralline and granitic islands. **IUCN** Least Concern.

The Asian House Gecko has a brown body with a mottled pattern of dark and light spots, and distinctive rings along the length of its tail. A nocturnal species that hides during the day and appears at night to hunt for small insects. The species displays a preference for urban environments and is is often found in association with human habitation. Similar to the Stump-toed Gecko (above), it makes a loud, repeating chirping sound.

Seychelles Sucker-tailed Gecko *Urocotyledon inexpectata* **LENGTH** 8cm

(Lezar disik)

INNER ISLANDS Most granitic islands. **IUCN** Least Concern.

A small brown gecko with a mottled pattern and heart-shaped pads at the ends of its toes, as its name suggests it has has a sucker at the end of its tail. It is a nocturnal species, and although it is common in the granitic islands, due to its cryptic nature it is rarely encountered.

Bronze-eyed Gecko *Ailuronyx seychellensis* **LENGTH** 20cm

(Lezar bronz)

INNER ISLANDS Most granitic islands. **IUCN** Least Concern.

A large gecko with variable colouration, from brown, to olive-grey, to black, the Bronze-eyed Gecko's body colour can be uniform or may be covered in a variety of markings. It is similar to the Dwarf Bronze Gecko (p. 52), but slightly larger and has a blunter snout. Largely nocturnal, this species feeds on insects and nectar. It is found in lowland forests and plantations and is threatened by habitat loss.

Stump-toed Gecko

Asian House Gecko

Seychelles Sucker-tailed Gecko

Bronze-eyed Gecko

Dwarf Bronze Gecko *Ailuronyx tachyscopaeus* LENGTH 15cm e

(Pti lezar bronz)

INNER ISLANDS Conception, La Digue, Mahé, Praslin, Silhouette.
IUCN Near Threatened.

This is a similar species to the Bronze-eyed Gecko (p. 50), with the same colouration, but differentiated by its smaller size and more pointed snout. It is found on the relatively large granitic islands, where it is nocturnal, feeding on insects.

Giant Bronze Gecko *Ailuronyx trachygaster* LENGTH 26cm e

(Gro lezar kokodmer)

INNER ISLANDS Praslin. **IUCN** Critically Endangered.

The Giant Bronze Gecko is the largest of the endemic gecko species and it is easily distinguished from the other bronze geckos. The body is olive to brown with flaps of loose skin behind the head. The large feet have toes with rounded pads that are white on the undersides. It is found in the Vallée de Mai on Praslin, where it lives high up in the Coco-de-mer palms.

Tiger Chameleon *Archaius tigris* LENGTH 20cm e

(Kameleon)

INNER ISLANDS Mahé, Praslin, Silhouette. **IUCN** Endangered.

A relatively small chameleon, this species generally grows to approximately 15cm in length. It varies in colour from bright yellow to white and grey, often with black markings and numerous spots. There is a distinctive pointed projection on the underside of its chin. It is found from sea level upwards, but prefers higher altitudes.

Seychelles Skink *Trachylepis sechellensis* LENGTH 22cm e

(Lezar mangouya)

INNER ISLANDS Bird, Denis and all granitic islands. **OUTER ISLANDS** Amirantes.
IUCN Least Concern.

The Seychelles Skink has a brown body with a lighter ventral surface; it is darker dorsally. There is a dark stripe along its side. A diurnal species, it is found in a variety of habitats, including close to human habitation. It can be inquisitive and often approaches closely in search of food. It lays a pair of eggs underground, and feeds on fruits, insects and other small reptiles, including those belonging to the genus *Phelsuma*.

Wright's Skink *Trachylepis wrightii* LENGTH 30cm e

(Lezar tengteng)

INNER ISLANDS Aride, Cousin, Cousine, Frégate. **IUCN** Vulnerable.

This large skink is found on cat- and rat-free islands, where it occurs in high numbers. It has a brown body that is paler on the underside. The species feeds on a variety of food sources, including fruits, insects and seabird eggs.

Dwarf Bronze Gecko

Giant Bronze Gecko

Tiger Chameleon

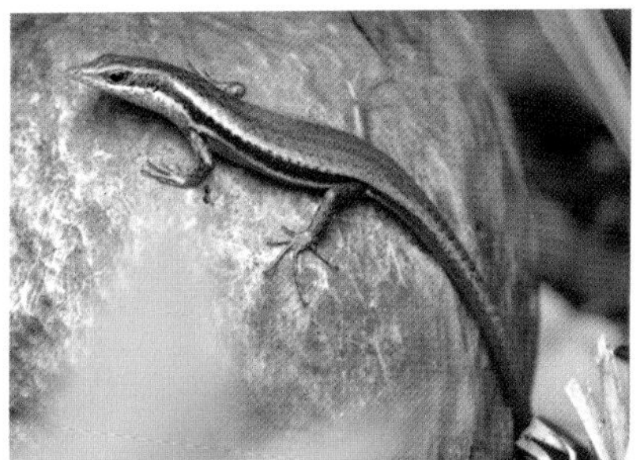
Seychelles Skink

Wright's Skink

Gardiner's Burrowing Skink *Pamelaescincus gardineri* **LENGTH** 14cm e
(Lezar later)

INNER ISLANDS Aride, Cousin, Cousine, Curieuse, Félicité, Frégate, La Digue, Mahé, Praslin, Silhouette. **IUCN** Near Threatened.

A small brown skink with short limbs, Gardiner's Burrowing Skink is slightly stockier than Brauer's Burrowing Skink (below). Found on many larger and several smaller granitic islands, it hides among the leaf litter particularly in native forests.

Brauer's Burrowing Skink *Janetaescincus braueri* **LENGTH** 12cm e
(Lezar later)

INNER ISLANDS Mahé, Silhouette. **IUCN** Endangered.

This small skink with short limbs and a thick tail has a dark brown body. It is rarely encountered, as it burrows into the leaf litter. It moves with a rapid wriggling motion.

Seychelles House Snake *Lamprophis geometricus* **LENGTH** 120cm e
(Koulev gri)

INNER ISLANDS Frégate, Mahé, Praslin, Silhouette. **IUCN** Endangered.

This thick-bodied, nocturnal snake prefers forest habitat. Its body is brown with dark stripes along the length and distinctive white stripes behind the eyes. It feeds on mice and lizards, killing them by constriction. It is harmless to humans. The species is commonly encountered on Frégate Island.

Seychelles Wolf Snake *Lycognathophis seychellensis* **LENGTH** 130cm e
(Koulev zonn)

INNER ISLANDS Aride, Cousine, Frégate, La Digue, Mahé, Praslin, Silhouette. **IUCN** Endangered.

A thin-bodied snake with variable colouration, a dark variation occurs alongside a golden one, which has a bright yellow underside. This snake is harmless to humans. It prefers forest habitat and can sometimes be encountered near human habitation.

Brahminy Blind Snake *Indotyphlops braminus* **LENGTH** 10cm i
(Koulev)

INNER ISLANDS Cerf, Cousine, Curieuse, Félicité, La Digue, Mahé, Praslin. **OUTER ISLANDS** Alphonse, Assumption. **IUCN** Least Concern.

A small, blind burrowing snake, this species has been introduced to many parts of the world. Is likely to be present on many of the granitic islands. It is similar in appearance to an earthworm, but possesses small scales. The species is known to be parthenogenetic. It is harmless to humans.

Gardiner's Burrowing Skink

Brauer's Burrowing Skink

Seychelles House Snake

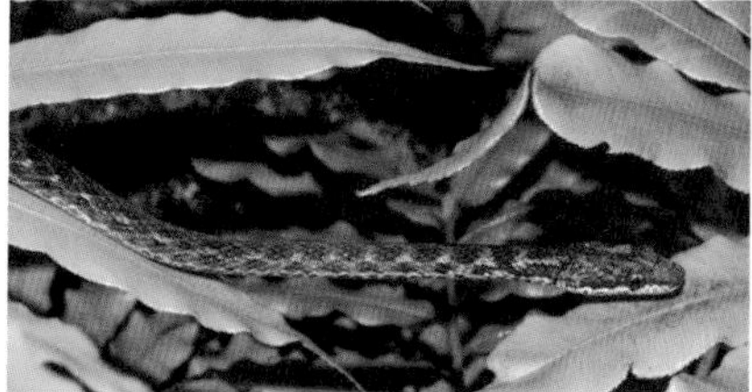

Seychelles Wolf Snake, dark variation

Seychelles Wolf Snake, golden variation

Brahminy Blind Snake

AMPHIBIANS

Amphibians require access to damp conditions to prevent them from drying out and enable oxygen exchange across their skin. Consequently, they are absent from Seychelles coralline islands. Unlike the dry outer islands, which are lacking in fresh water, the granitic islands of Seychelles provide the perfect conditions for amphibians to thrive. There are currently 14 species of amphibian in Seychelles, 13 of which are endemic. Of these, six species are frogs and the remaining eight are caecilians. The forests of Mahé, Praslin and Silhouette provide the best opportunity to see many of these species, particularly after rain or at higher altitudes.

FROGS

Of the six species of frog found in Seychelles, four belong to the family Sooglossidae. These are some of the smallest frogs in the world and are terrestrial breeders, meaning they do not require water for larval development. Their population size is unknown, but due to a limited range, they are under threat from habitat loss, introduced species, climate change and diseases. The other two frog species, both restricted to the inner granitic islands, are the endemic Seychelles Tree Frog and the introduced Mascarene Frog (below).

Mascarene Frog *Ptychadena mascareniensis* **LENGTH** 5cm i

(Grenuiy)

INNER ISLANDS Granitic islands. **IUCN** Not Evaluated.

This mottled brown, ground-dwelling frog with dark striping on the legs and back is the only non-endemic amphibian species in Seychelles. It is found in a variety of habitats, including close to human habitation. Its eggs are laid into standing water and hatch within a few days.

Seychelles Tree Frog *Tachycnemis seychellensis* **LENGTH** 5cm e

(Krapo)

INNER ISLANDS La Digue, Mahé, Praslin, Silhouette. **IUCN** Least Concern.

An endemic nocturnal tree frog, this species is found close to ponds and streams. Males are brown to red, while females are larger and green. Both sexes have vertical pupils and distinctive toe-pads. Although the species favours mid-altitude forests, it is found in a variety of habitats.

Mascarene Frog

♀

♂

Seychelles Tree Frog

Gardiner's Pygmy Frog *Sechellophryne gardineri* **LENGTH** 1.3cm **e**

(Grenuiy nen)

INNER ISLANDS Mahé, Silhouette. **IUCN** Endangered.

The smallest of Seychelles frogs, Gardiner's Pygmy Frog is found in mid- to high-altitude forests. It often hides amongst leaf litter or on moss-covered rocks. In areas that support high densities of endemic palms, Gardiner's Pygmy Frog can sometimes be found on the palm fronds. It is variable in colour, ranging from tan to reddish-brown with dark sides to the head and body. Males make a distinctive high-pitched call. The species is the most commonly encountered of the Sooglossid frogs.

Seychelles Pygmy Frog *Sooglossus sechellensis* **LENGTH** 2cm **e**

(Grenuiy nen)

INNER ISLANDS Mahé, Praslin, Silhouette. **IUCN** Endangered.

The body and legs of the Seychelles Pygmy Frog are golden brown with dark spots and markings. It is larger than Gardiner's Pygmy Frog (above), but smaller than Thomasset's Frog (below). It is restricted to undisturbed forests, where it hides in the leaf litter.

Thomasset's Frog *Sooglossus thomasetti* **LENGTH** 5cm **e**

(Grenuiy nen)

INNER ISLANDS Mahé, Silhouette. **IUCN** Critically Endangered.

The largest of Seychelles' endemic frog species, Thomasset's Frog is also the rarest. The body is gold to brown on top with dark markings, and the eyes are golden with black pupils. Its eggs, which are laid in rock crevices, do not have a larval stage and instead tiny miniature versions of the adult hatch fully developed. The species is restricted to undisturbed areas 350m above sea level, where it is active at night. Thomasset's Frog is threatened by habitat destruction, invasive species and climate change.

Silhouette Palm Frog *Sooglossus pipilodryas* **LENGTH** 1.5cm **e**

(Grenuiy nen)

INNER ISLANDS Silhouette. **IUCN** Critically Endangered.

First described as a new species in 2002, the Silhouette Palm Frog is restricted to the island of Silhouette. It is similar in appearance to Gardiner's Pygmy Frog (above), but has a distinctive dark diamond shape on the back. It is found in leaf litter and on endemic palms.

Gardiner's Pygmy Frog

Seychelles Pygmy Frog

Thomasset's Frog

Silhouette Palm Frog

CAECILIANS

There are eight species of endemic caecilian in Seychelles, all restricted to the granitic islands. These worm-like, limbless amphibians are burrowing animals that grow to approximately 30cm and are found in leaf litter or in fresh water. The eyes are very small and there is a pair of sensory organs near the snout. The different species are similar in appearance and identification can be difficult. In addition, due to their behaviour and habitat preference, caecilians are rarely encountered, though they are widespread on the larger islands.

Little Praslin Caecilian *Hypogeophis pti* LENGTH 1.2cm e

INNER ISLANDS Praslin. **IUCN** Not Evaluated.

A small caecilian growing to 1.2cm in length, the Little Praslin Caecilian has fewer vertebrae than any other caecilian species. It was first identified in 2013 prior to being described in 2017 and is found only on Praslin Island, with its restricted range making it susceptible to extinction.

Frigate Island Caecilian *Hypogeophis rostratus* LENGTH 35cm e

INNER ISLANDS Cerf Island, Curieuse, Félicité, Frégate, La Digue, Mahé, Praslin, Silhouette, Ste Anne. **IUCN** Least Concern.

One of the more widespread of Seychelles caecilians, the Frigate Island Caecilian is found on most of the larger granitic islands. It has a dark body, paler ventrally and with numerous annuli. The small head is pointed and the eyes are covered by skin. Unusually for caecilians, water is not essential to this species for breeding and eggs are laid in clutches, which the female coils her body around until they are ready to hatch.

Stejneger's Caecilian *Grandisonia alternans* LENGTH 30cm e

INNER ISLANDS Félicité, Frégate, La Digue, Mahé, Praslin, Silhouette, Ste Anne. **IUCN** Least Concern.

This common caecilian has a dark body that becomes grey in colour towards the head. It is found in a variety of habitats, including disturbed areas, where it occurs in the leaf litter and burrows in wet soil.

Little Praslin

Frigate Island Caecilian

Stejneger's Caecilian

FRESHWATER FISH

Due to the islands' isolation and limited freshwater habitats, freshwater fish are not well represented in Seychelles and are only present within the granitic islands. Very few solely inhabit fresh water, while several species are found in the brackish environments of coastal mangroves. The streams of the larger granitic islands are also home to a variety of introduced species.

Eel *Anguilla bicolor bicolor* LENGTH 100cm n

(Ange)

INNER ISLANDS Curieuse, La Digue, Mahé, Praslin, Silhouette.
IUCN Near Threatened.
This large, thick-bodied eel is found in streams and wetlands on the larger granitic islands. It can grow to more than 1m in length, and feeds on small crabs and fish. Adult eels return to oceanic breeding sites.

Spangled Gudgeon *Ophiocara porocephala* LENGTH 34cm n

(Makanbale letet ron)

INNER ISLANDS Granitic islands. **IUCN** Least Concern.
The Spangled Gudgeon is a dark-bodied fish with a large head and yellow margin on the anal and second dorsal fins. It prefers brackish water and is often associated with mangroves, where it can be found living among the root systems. The Spangled Gudgeon is also common in the canals that pass through urban environments.

Mozambique Tilapia *Oreochromis mossambicus* LENGTH 35cm i

(Tilapya)

INNER ISLANDS La Digue, Mahé, Praslin, Silhouette. **IUCN** Vulnerable.
Originally from south-east Africa, the Mozambique Tilapia has been widely introduced and is described as one of the 100 worst invasive species in the world. The adults are green to black, with males darker in colour than females. During breeding, males excavate depressions into which females lay eggs.

Eel

Spangled Gudgeon

Mozambique Tilapia

Golden Panchax *Pachypanchax playfairii* **LENGTH** 10cm e
(Gourzon)

INNER ISLANDS La Digue, Mahé, Praslin, Silhouette. **IUCN** Data Deficient.
The Golden Panchax is found in a variety of freshwater habitats on the larger granitic islands, including in high-altitude streams. While the juveniles are dull in colour, the adults exhibit metallic red-and-green markings, with the males being particularly colourful.

Guppy *Poecilia reticulata* **LENGTH** 4cm i
(Milyon)

INNER ISLANDS Mahé. **IUCN** Least Concern.
Native to northern South America and the Caribbean, guppies are one of the world's most widely distributed tropical fish, and the introduced species has established itself in the low- and mid-altitude streams of Mahé. The males are brightly coloured, while the females are silver to brown with a rounded belly.

Golden Panchax

Guppy

SNAILS & SLUGS

The terrestrial molluscs of Seychelles are a very diverse group, with about 60 species of snail and slug having been identified. The majority of these occur within the granitic islands, which receive more rainfall than other areas. However, molluscs are also found on the coralline islands, and on the remote islands of and adjacent to Aldabra atoll. Many of the terrestrial molluscs on the larger granitic islands are endemic. They are easily found in mid- to high-altitude forests, particularly during the rainy season, when they attach to endemic palms.

Aldabra Banded Snail *Rhachistia aldabrae* **LENGTH** 1.5cm ⓔ

OUTER ISLANDS Aldabra atoll. **IUCN** Critically Endangered.

A large snail endemic to Aldabra atoll, this species lives on native scrub. The distinctive dark purple shell has pink bands. Thought to be extinct due to climate change, a population of the snails was rediscovered in 2014 with further populations identified since.

Coco-de-mer Snail *Stylodonta studeriana* **LENGTH** 7cm ⓔ

(Leskargo)

INNER ISLANDS Praslin. **IUCN** Endangered.

A large endemic snail associated with Coco-de-mer palms, this species is found in the Vallée de Mai and neighbouring forests. It has a round and flattened, brown-yellow shell with a white lip, and a brown brown body. The Coco-de-mer Snail is threatened by habitat destruction and introduced species, such as the Yellow Crazy Ants (*Anoplolepis graccilipes*).

Seychelles Snail *Stylodonta unidentata* **LENGTH** 5cm ⓔ

(Kourpa)

INNER ISLANDS Conception, Curieuse, La Digue, Mahé, Praslin, Silhouette.
IUCN Vulnerable.

Similar in appearance to the Coco-de-mer Snail (above), with a brown to yellow, flattened circular shell, the Seychelles Snail is slightly smaller and is found on a number of the granitic islands. It prefers forests with endemic palms, where it is active by day.

Aldabra Banded Snail

Coco-de-mer Snail

Seychelles Snail

Black Dancing Snail *Pachnodus niger* **LENGTH** 2cm e

(Kolimason)

INNER ISLANDS Mahé, Praslin. **IUCN** Endangered.

A small black snail with a black shell and orange lip, the Black Dancing Snail is found in mid- to high-altitude forests on Mahé and Praslin, where it can be seen after rain. It performs a characteristic 'dancing' motion if the shell is lightly touched.

Praslin Snail *Pachnodus praslinus* **LENGTH** 2cm e

(Kolimason)

INNER ISLANDS Praslin. **IUCN** Vulnerable.

This small snail is endemic to the island of Praslin. It has a pale shell with dark rings on the whorls. The body is pale cream in colour, with grey to black sensory organs. It is associated with palm forests.

Silhouette Snail *Pachnodus silhouettanus* **LENGTH** 2cm e

(Kolimason)

INNER ISLANDS Silhouette. **IUCN** Near Threatened.

This small endemic land snail is confined to the island of Silhouette. It has a mottled yellow to dark brown shell, and a grey to brown body with dark sensory organs. It favours mid- to high-altitude palm forests.

African Land Snail *Achatina immaculata* **LENGTH** 15cm i

(Kourpa)

INNER & OUTER ISLANDS Granitic and coralline islands. **IUCN** Least Concern.

The African Land Snail is a large, predominantly brown snail with a conical shell that has wavy, variably coloured bands on it. An introduced pest species, it feeds on food crops and probably competes with native snail species. It is common in gardens on the larger granitic islands.

Seychelles Slug *Filicaulis seychellensis* **LENGTH** 15cm e

(Lalangmelanni)

INNER ISLANDS Mahé, Praslin, Silhouette. **IUCN** Least Concern.

A large slug, this species is variable in colour but all white on Praslin, where it feeds on the male flowers of Coco-de-mer palms. It is greyish-brown to brown on Mahé and Silhouette, where it prefers mid- to high-altitude palm forests.

Black Dancing Snail

Praslin Snail

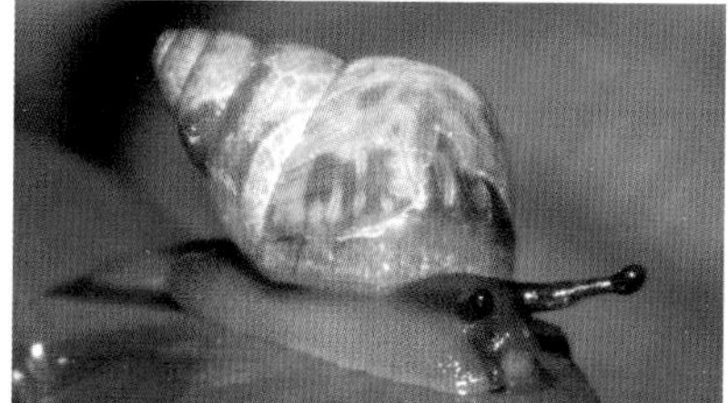
Silhouette Snail

African Land Snail

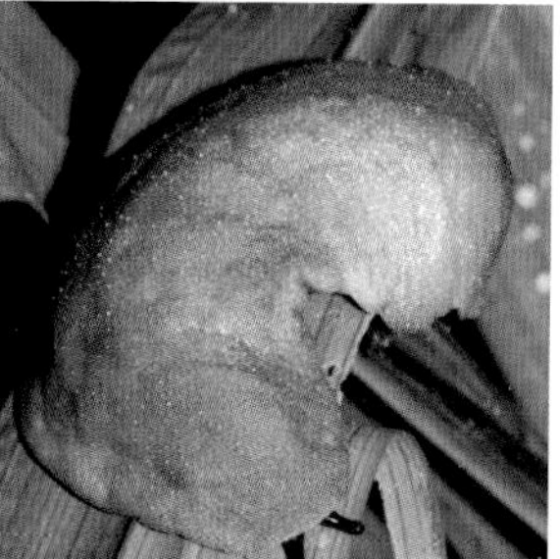
Seychelles Slug

CRUSTACEANS

A large number of crustaceans, including shellfish, is found in Seychelles. The phylum includes crabs, lobsters, shrimps and barnacles. They can be further divided into marine, freshwater and terrestrial species. Seychelles marine crabs are a diverse group; most are native to Seychelles and can be found on the beaches and in coastal zones of the majority of islands. Freshwater crabs and crayfish are found in rivers and streams of the granitic islands from sea level up to high altitudes. Terrestrial crabs include hermit crabs and the Coconut Crab, which scavenge along beaches.

Mangrove Crab *Cardisoma carnifex* LENGTH 20cm (carapace size) n

(Tyangoman)

INNER & OUTER ISLANDS Most islands. **IUCN** Data Deficient.

This large land crab is brown to orange above and pale below. Males have enlarged claws, one bigger than the other, which they raise when threatened. A coastal species, as the name would suggest, the Mangrove Crab is often found near mangrove forests where it can be very common. The crabs reside in burrows by day, especially in muddy habitats, emerging at night to feed on vegetation and debris. Leaves of the White Mangrove *Avicennia marina* form a large part of the crab's diet.

Coconut Crab *Birgus latro* LENGTH To 60cm (in width) n

(Sipay)

INNER ISLANDS Recorded very rarely in the granitic islands. **OUTER ISLANDS** Rare in the Amirantes island group. Abundant at Aldabra atoll, Asomption, Cosmoledo atoll, Astove and Farquhar atoll. **IUCN** Vulnerable.

The Coconut Crab is the largest terrestrial crab in the world. It is very rare in the granitic islands, where it has probably been over-hunted. The species reportedly takes more than 10 years to reach sexual maturity, making it very vulnerable to human over-exploitation. It has a broad body with a pair of large pincers used for opening coconuts and other food sources. It is known to steal items from humans, hence its alternative name of 'Robber Crab'. Although often associated with coconut plantations, Coconut Crabs do not require coconuts to survive. Their diet consists of a variety of food items, including coconuts, tortoise and sea turtle hatchlings, as well as dead seabirds. Two colour variations occur, an orange-red type and a purple-blue variation. The crabs are predominantly nocturnal, remaining in a burrow during the day.

Mangrove Crab

Coconut Crab

Coconut Crab, orange-red colour variation

Purple Hermit Crab *Coenobita brevimanus* **LENGTH** 15cm (carapace size) n

(Solda)

INNER & OUTER ISLANDS Most islands. **IUCN** Not Evaluated.

This large terrestrial hermit crab has a purple body and black eyes. It retreats into its shell when disturbed. A mainly nocturnal species, it emerges at night to feed on vegetation and animal debris. It inhabits beach-crest vegetation and coastal areas.

Red Hermit Crab *Coenobita perlatus* **LENGTH** 6cm (carapace size) n

(Solda)

INNER & OUTER ISLANDS Most islands. **IUCN** Not Evaluated.

This medium-sized hermit crab ranges from pale cream when young to bright reddish-orange when adult. The eyes are black and the antennae are bright orange. It inhabits beach-crest vegetation, emerging to feed in the late afternoons and early evenings.

Pale Hermit Crab *Coenobita rugosus* **LENGTH** 4cm (carapace size) n

(Solda)

INNER & OUTER ISLANDS Most islands. **IUCN** Not Evaluated.

The smallest and most abundant of the native hermit crabs, the Pale Hermit Crab is most prevalent on uninhabited islands. It is pale grey in colour with black eyes and bent antennae, and is active during the morning and at night, when it scavenges for food above the high-water mark.

Orange Land Crab *Geograpsus crinipes* **LENGTH** 4.5cm (carapace size) n

(Karkasay)

INNER & OUTER ISLANDS Most islands. **IUCN** Not Evaluated.

The carapace and legs of the Orange Land Crab are uniformly orange-brown, while the eyes are pale with dark centres. The body is flattened and the legs are relatively long. The species is associated with rocky shores, where it is most active at dusk and dawn.

Horned Ghost Crab *Ocypode ceratophthalmus*

LENGTH 4.5cm (carapace size) n

(Loulou grangalo)

INNER & OUTER ISLANDS All islands. **IUCN** Not Evaluated.

Because it runs backwards and forwards on the foreshore just above the water line, the Horned Ghost Crab is the most commonly encountered crab on Seychelles beaches. It has a pale green body that becomes yellow at the joints, and distinctive pale orange horns above the eyes. It scavenges and preys on a variety of plants and animals, including hatchling sea turtles.

Purple Hermit Crab

Red Hermit Crab

Pale Hermit Crab

Orange Land Crab

Horned Ghost Crab

Smooth-handed Ghost Crab *Ocypode cordimanus*

LENGTH 4.5cm (carapace size) n
(Loulou grangalo)
INNER & OUTER ISLANDS All islands. **IUCN** Not Evaluated.

A stocky ghost crab, the Smooth-handed Ghost Crab has a deep body and lacks horns above the eyes. It is grey to purple-brown in colour, with blue-grey claws. The crabs prefer the upper beach crest, where they construct burrows, spend much of their time underground, and scavenge for food both above and below ground (including turtle eggs and hatchlings still in the nest).

Red-eyed Crab *Eriphia sebana* **LENGTH** 6cm (carapace size) n

(Loulou)
INNER & OUTER ISLANDS Most islands. **IUCN** Not Evaluated.

The Red-eyed Crab has a rounded carapace with small granules on the surface. The body and legs are brown to purple in colour, while the eyes are bright red. It is commonly associated with rocks and rubble areas of the intertidal zone. The species is believed to be toxic and is not consumed locally.

Red Rock Crab *Neosarmatium meinerti* **LENGTH** 5cm (carapace size) n

(Loulou)
INNER & OUTER ISLANDS Most islands. **IUCN** Not Evaluated.

The Red Rock Crab is one of the most common crabs of the intertidal zone. The carapace is purple to black, the legs are dark grey with numerous hairs, and the claws are bright red, becoming orange towards the tips. The crabs burrow in mud in mangroves and along the banks of streams. It occurs in large numbers along the streams that run through Seychelles' capital city, Victoria.

Sally-lightfoot Crab *Grapsus tenuicrustatus* **LENGTH** 7cm (carapace size) n

(Karkasay)
INNER & OUTER ISLANDS All islands. **IUCN** Not Evaluated.

This common crab species is often seen scurrying over rocks in the littoral zone. It is extremely skittish and will quickly disappear under a rock or into the water when approached. The flattened body is usually dark green to black with lighter green markings, and the claws and legs are sometimes reddish. It is an intertidal species and feeds on algae.

Smooth-handed Ghost Crab

Red-eyed Crab

Red Rock Crab

Sally-lightfoot Crab

Tetragonal Fiddler Crab *Gelasimus tetragonon*

LENGTH 2cm (carapace size) n
(Krab semafot)
INNER & OUTER ISLANDS Most islands. **IUCN** Not Evaluated.
Female Tetragonal Fiddler Crabs are dull black in colour, while males have a turquoise carapace and a greatly enlarged pincer used for signalling to other crabs. The crabs are found near burrows in muddy substrate, where they feed on organic matter.

Scribbled Fiddler Crab *Austruca occidentalis*

LENGTH 1.5cm (carapace size) n
(Krab semafot)
INNER & OUTER ISLANDS Most islands. **IUCN** Not Evaluated.
This common fiddler crab within the granitic islands has a grey to black carapace with lighter scribbled markings. The limbs are grey to brown, with the enlarged pincer of the male being pale pink. The species inhabits muddy areas in mangroves, where it builds burrows.

Praslin Freshwater Crab *Seychellum alluaudi*

LENGTH 4cm (carapace size) e
(Krab larivyer)
INNER ISLANDS La Digue, Praslin. **IUCN** Vulnerable.
This small crab with a uniform orange to brown body and legs is endemic to the islands of Praslin and La Digue, where it is found from sea level to high altitudes. Genetic analyses of freshwater crabs found on Mahé/Frégate and Silhouette have shown them to be separate species. The crabs burrow into the banks of streams and rivers.

Crayfish *Macrobrachium* spp. **LENGTH** 20cm n

(Kamaron grolebra)
INNER ISLANDS Curieuse, Mahé, Praslin, Silhouette. **IUCN** Not Evaluated.
Several crayfish species belonging to the genus *Macrobrachium* are found in the streams of the granitic islands. *M. lar* is one of the larger species and has an orange to brown body with long, slender forelimbs.

Caridina Shrimp *Caridina typus* **LENGTH** 5cm n

(Sevret)
INNER ISLANDS La Digue, Mahé, Praslin, Silhouette. **IUCN** Least Concern.
This native shrimp is variable in appearance, with colours that may change depending on its environment. It is found in rivers and streams on the larger granitic islands, where it feeds by grazing on detritus.

Tetragonal Fiddler Crab

Scribbled Fiddler Crab

Praslin Freshwater Crab

Crayfish

Caridina Shrimp

MILLIPEDES & CENTIPEDES

The subphylum Myriapoda contains approximately 13,000 species made up of several closely related groups. It contains both the millipedes and centipedes, which are represented by several species in Seychelles, the most conspicuous of which are the giant species. They prefer damp conditions are often found within decaying organic matter, such as fallen tree trunks. Millipedes have two pairs of legs on each body segment, while centipedes, which are much flatter, only have one pair per segment.

Seychelles Giant Millipede *Sechelleptus seychellarum* **LENGTH** 30cm e

(Milpat)

INNER ISLANDS Granitic islands. **IUCN** Endangered.

Adult Seychelles Giant Millipedes are dark brown to black with a segmented body and shiny appearance, while juveniles tend to be red to brown. The millipede is more active at night, when it comes out to fed on detritus. It is most common on rat-free islands, although it can also be easily observed on Silhouette Island.

Giant Centipede *Scolopendra subspinipes* **LENGTH** 20cm n

(Sanpye)

INNER ISLANDS Most islands. **IUCN** Not Evaluated

This large, flattened centipede is common throughout the tropics. It has a brown segmented body with numerous legs projecting outwards, a pair of straight antennae and large jaws. It is capable of inflicting a painful bite and feeds on invertebrates, small lizards and decaying material. The species is often found near human habitation.

Seychelles Giant Millipede

Giant Centipede

SPIDERS & SCORPIONS

The arachnids make up a class of arthropods with more than 100,000 species. They include the spiders and scorpions, and the majority of them have eight legs. Seychelles is well represented by the true spiders, with several species found on the granitic and coralline islands. Seychelles scorpions comprise three species, none of which are considered to be dangerous to humans.

Giant Black Scorpion *Chiromachus ochropus* LENGTH 10cm n

(Skorpyon nwanr)

INNER ISLANDS Frégate, Praslin. **IUCN** Vulnerable.

While the Giant Black Scorpion may still be present on other granitic islands, it is currently known from Frégate Island. A nocturnal species, which hides during the day, this brown to black scorpion with large pincers feeds on other invertebrates.

Tailless Whipscorpion *Charinus seychellarum* LENGTH 1cm (body size) e

(Tarantin arme)

INNER ISLANDS Felicite, Frégate, Long Island, Mahé, North Island, Praslin, Silhouette. **IUCN** Vulnerable.

A whip spider with a brown body and antennae, the Tailless Whipscorpion's front limbs are enlarged and bent in front of the body. A harmless nocturnal species, it is found on a number of the granitic islands.

Red-legged Orb-weaver *Trichonephila inaurata* LENGTH 10cm n

(Bibouk)

INNER ISLANDS Bird, Denis and granitic islands. **OUTER ISLANDS** Aldabra atoll and coralline islands. **IUCN** Least Concern.

A very common spider found throughout Seychelles, the Red-legged Orb-weaver can be seen sitting in the middle of its very large web. Females are larger than males and have conspicuous red-and-black banded legs. The spiders feed on a variety of insects.

Crab Spider *Damastes validus* LENGTH 12cm e

(Bibouk)

INNER & OUTER ISLANDS Coralline and granitic islands. **IUCN** Least Concern.

A large, hairy spider with a brown body, the Crab Spider is endemic to Seychelles, and is found in forested areas and close to human habitation. It does not build a web, preferring to make a shelter among leaves using silk-like thread.

Giant Black Scorpion

Tailless Whipscorpion

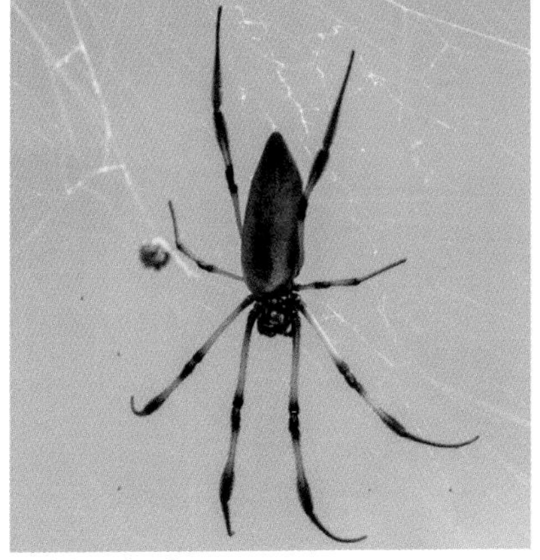

Red-legged Orb-weaver

Crab Spider

Humped Spider *Zosis geniculata* **LENGTH** 1.2cm (n)

INNER ISLANDS Granitic islands. **IUCN** Not Evaluated.

Often found near human habitation, the Humped Spider builds webs in outhouses and the roofs of rural constructions. The abdomen is pale while the legs are banded, alternating between cream and dark brown. The two front legs are elongated.

Common Bark Spider *Caerostris sexcuspidata* **LENGTH** 3cm (n)

INNER & OUTER ISLANDS Aldabra atoll, coralline and granitic islands. **IUCN** Not Evaluated.

Restricted to the east coast of Africa and the western Indian Ocean, this orb spider builds large webs. The body is grey to brown with horny projections, which aid in camouflage. The legs are brown and hairy.

Pantropic Jumping Spider *Plexippus paykulli* **LENGTH** 1cm (i)

INNER ISLANDS Granitic islands. **IUCN** Not Evaluated.

The female Pantropic Jumping Spider is grey brown in appearance and slightly larger than the male. The male has a distinctive white stripe down the centre of a dark carapace and abdomen. The species is usually found in human habitation.

Gray Wall Jumping Spider *Menemerus bivittatus* **LENGTH** 0.9cm (i)

INNER ISLANDS Granitic islands. **IUCN** Not Evaluated.

This common jumping spider is found throughout the tropics. Males have a dark dorsal stripe with a paler stripe on each side of the abdomen. The female is usually paler and both sexes have banding on the legs.

Golden Jumping Spider *Cosmophasis lami* **LENGTH** 0.5cm (i)

INNER ISLANDS Coralline and granitic islands. **IUCN** Not Evaluated.

A small but common jumping spider, this species is usually found on the leaves of plants, where it mimics ants. The body is orange to golden and the legs are pale and covered in hairs. It feeds on a variety of small insects.

Short-horn Kite Spider *Gasteracantha sanguinolenta* **LENGTH** 1cm (n)

INNER & OUTER ISLANDS Aldabra atoll, coralline and granitic islands. **IUCN** Not Evaluated.

This spiny orb-weaver has relatively short spines on its abdomen. It tends to have a red-and-white abdomen, although the colours can be variable, including between sexes. It builds a small web suspended between vegetation.

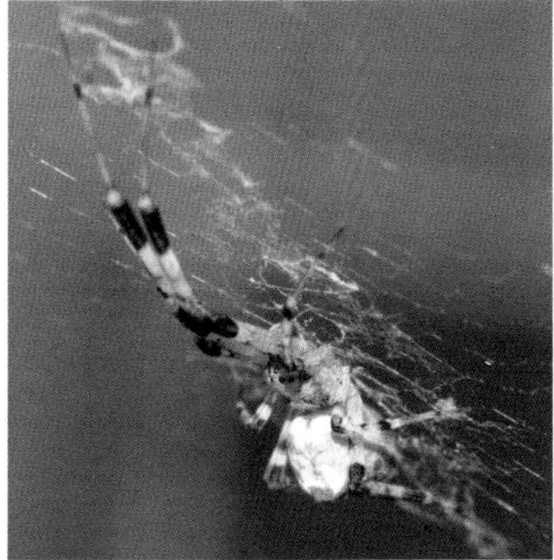
Humped Spider

Common Bark Spider

Pantropic Jumping Spider

Gray Wall Jumping Spider

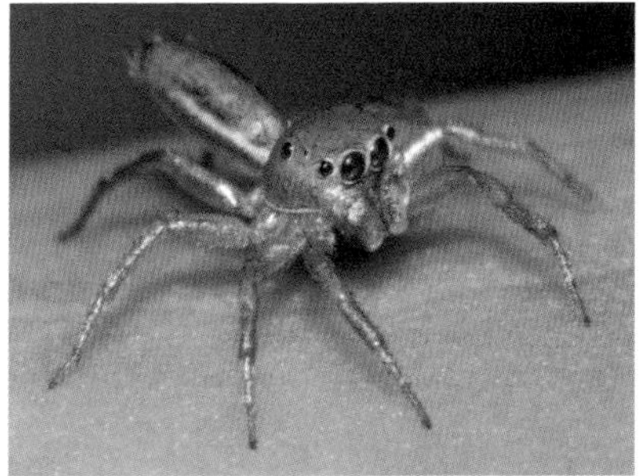
Golden Jumping Spider

Short-horn Kite Spider

DRAGONFLIES & DAMSELFLIES

The Odonata order comprises the dragonflies and damselflies – one of the oldest groups of insects, which do not resemble any other existing order. They have long, slender abdomens and a pair of similarly sized wings. Their heads contain a pair of very large compound eyes. Adult dragonflies normally perch with their wings flattened, while the wings of damselflies remain folded when at rest. Both dragonflies and damselflies have aquatic larvae, and the adults can often be seen close to marshes and wetlands.

Orange Damselfly *Ceriagrion glabrum* LENGTH 3.5cm n

(Sigal)

INNER ISLANDS Coralline and granitic islands. **IUCN** Least Concern.

Widespread throughout Africa, this distinctive damselfly has green eyes. The Orange Damselfly displays sexual dimorphism and males have a bright orange body, while females are brown. It is often found near ponds and marshes on the coastal plateaux, where it can be seen resting on the tips of plants.

Blue-tailed Damselfly *Ischnura senegalensis* LENGTH 3.5cm n

(Sigal)

INNER & OUTER ISLANDS Aldabra atoll, coralline and granitic islands. **IUCN** Least Concern.

This small damselfly has variable colouration depending on sex and life stage. Older males and females have a black abdomen and upper surface of thorax. The sides of the thorax are green. The Blue-tailed Damselfly is one of the most wide-ranging dragonflies in the world. It inhabits the marshes of coastal plateaux and is also found near polluted standing water in urban areas.

Chalky Percher *Diplacodes trivialis* LENGTH 4.5cm n

(Sigal)

INNER ISLANDS Granitic islands. **IUCN** Least Concern.

The Chalky Percher is a small dragonfly with blue eyes. Males have a blue thorax and abdomen, while females have a black abdomen with yellow spots. The species is associated with ponds and marshes on coastal plateaux and will even breed in drainage ditches.

Orange Damselfly

Blue-tailed Damselfly

Chalky Percher

Seychelles Skimmer *Orthetrum stemmale* **LENGTH** 4.5cm n
(Sigal)

INNER ISLANDS Granitic islands. **IUCN** Least Concern.

A small dragonfly with metallic blue eyes, adults have paired yellow spots behind the head, and on the thorax and abdomen. The abdomen becomes more blue in mature adults. The species is associated with ponds and marshes on coastal plateaux.

Phantom Flutterer *Rhyothemis semihyalina* **LENGTH** 5cm n
(Sigal)

INNER & OUTER ISLANDS Aldabra atoll, coralline and granitic islands.
IUCN Least Concern.

The body of this dragonfly is almost black, and there are dark purple patches on the wings close to the body. It has a characteristic fluttering flight and can be seen near wetlands and waterways.

PRAYING MANTISES

Praying mantises are ambush predators, relying on their camouflage to capture their prey. Their large forelegs have rows of spines for grasping prey items, and are held in front of the body in a characteristic 'praying' posture. They have a large, triangular head with compound eyes. There are two species of praying mantis in Seychelles.

Madagascan Marbled Mantis *Polyspilota aeruginosa* **LENGTH** 10cm n

INNER & OUTER ISLANDS Aldabra atoll, coralline and granitic islands.
IUCN Least Concern.

This common mantid often enters buildings at night, attracted by the light. Colour variations include grey, brown and occasionally green. The insects prey on a variety of food sources, including other insects and small geckos.

Seychelles Mantis *Polyspilota seychelliana* **LENGTH** 10cm e

INNER ISLANDS Granitic islands. **IUCN** Least Concern.

This species is less common that the Madagascan Marbled Mantis (above), and prefers mid- to high-altitude forested areas with native vegetation. The large head and compound eyes are green, as is the rest of the body. The abdomen tends to be broad and flattened.

Seychelles Skimmer

Phantom Flutterer

Madagascan Marbled Mantis

Seychelles Mantis

STICK & LEAF INSECTS

The phasmids – which include stick and leaf insects – are a group of insects that rely heavily on camouflage to avoid detection. They are herbivores and are confined to the larger granitic islands. Many species resemble part of a plant, such as a leaf or twig. There are five species of stick insect and one species of leaf insect in Seychelles.

Gardiner's Stick Insect *Carausius gardineri* **LENGTH** 6cm e

(Seval dibwa)

INNER ISLANDS Mahé, Silhouette. **IUCN** Least Concern.

Found on the larger granitic islands, the body of Gardiner's Stick Insect is either brown or bright green, enabling it to blend in with its background. The eyes are a reddish colour, and females differ from males by having a broader body.

Seychelles Stick Insect *Carausius seychellensis* **LENGTH** 10cm e

(Seval dibwa)

INNER ISLANDS Curieuse, Concéption, La Digue, Felicité, Mahé, Praslin, Silhouette. **IUCN** Least Concern.

The Seychelles Stick Insect has a brown body with two small spines at the top of the head between the eyes. It feeds on ferns, and in particular *Nephrolepis biserrata*, on which it can often be found. It prefers mid- to high-altitude forests.

Seychelles Winged Stick Insect *Graeffea seychellensis* **LENGTH** 10cm e

(Seval dibwa)

INNER ISLANDS Mahé, Praslin, Silhouette. **IUCN** Endangered.

The Seychelles Winged Stick Insect is the only winged species of stick insect found in Seychelles. Individuals are either green or brown, and occur in mid- to high-altitude forests, as well as in gardens close to human habitation.

Leaf Insect *Phyllium bioculatum* **LENGTH** 8cm n

(Mous fey)

INNER ISLANDS Granitic islands. **IUCN** Least Concern.

The Leaf Insect has a flattened body with green to brown colouration and veins resembling that of a leaf, providing excellent camouflage. It is associated with introduced fruit trees, where it is slow moving, relying on its camouflage to avoid predators.

Gardiner's Stick Insect

Seychelles Stick Insect

Seychelles Winged Stick Insect

Leaf Insect

GRASSHOPPERS & CRICKETS

Grasshoppers and crickets belong to a diverse order of insects, the Orthoptera. They are usually distinguished from each other by the length of their antennae (grasshoppers having the much shorter antennae of the two). The Orthoptera have sturdy bodies and large heads. The hindlegs are large, enabling them to jump long distances.

Seychelles Monkey Grasshopper *Euschmidtia cruciformis*

LENGTH 2cm ⓔ

INNER ISLANDS Mahé, Silhouette. **IUCN** Least Concern.

The Seychelles Monkey Grasshopper has a green to brown body with large eyes and legs, which stick out at right angles to the abdomen. It is a flightless species and the sexes can be identified, as the female is larger than the male. It is found in mid-altitude forests and scrub on the larger granitic islands, where it feeds on both native and introduced vegetation.

Seychelles Palm Grasshopper *Enoplotettix gardineri* **LENGTH** 4cm ⓔ

INNER ISLANDS Curieuse, Mahé, Praslin, Silhouette. **IUCN** Endangered.

The Seychelles Palm Grasshopper has a bright green body with striped yellow-and-purple to black wings. Individuals with blue on the hindlegs are males, while those with red are females. The species is found on the larger granitic islands, where it is associated with native palms. Currently listed as an endangered species, the Seychelles Palm Grasshopper is threatened by habitat degradation and the introduction of non-native vegetation.

Seychelles Cricket *Seychellesia patelllifera* **LENGTH** 5cm ⓔ

INNER ISLANDS Mahé, Silhouette. **IUCN** Endangered.

The Seychelles Cricket has a predominantly brown body with a pale yellow streak down each side. Found on the larger granitic islands, where it prefers mid-altitude forests, it is associated with native palms.

Green Bush Cricket *Pelerinus rostratus* **LENGTH** 5cm ⓔ

(Kasbol)

INNER ISLANDS Granitic islands and Denis. **IUCN** Least Concern.

A common bush cricket that is often found near human habitation, the Green Bush Cricket frequently flies into homes in the evenings, attracted by the lights. The body and small head are green, while the large green wings remain folded against the insect's sides. It feeds on the leaves of both native and introduced trees.

Seychelles Monkey Grasshopper

Seychelles Palm Grasshopper

Seychelles Cricket

Green Bush Cricket

BEETLES

Beetles belong to the order Coleoptera, which represents the most diverse group of animals worldwide, with more than 370,000 species described so far. Many beetles have two pairs of wings; the forewings (elytra) are a pair of hard shells, which protect the more delicate hindwings folded underneath. There are numerous species of beetle in Seychelles, and the group remains understudied locally.

Father Filibert's Beetle *Calirrhipis philiberti* LENGTH 2cm e

(Makabe plim)

INNER ISLANDS Coralline and granitic islands. **IUCN** Data Deficient.

A predominantly brown beetle with characteristic antennae, which are divided into several strands, Father Filibert's Beetle is found in a variety of habitats. It occasionally enters human habitation, attracted by the lights.

Frégate Island Giant Tenebrionid Beetle *Polposipus herculeanus* LENGTH 3cm e

(Bib arme)

INNER ISLANDS Frégate. **IUCN** Vulnerable.

This beetle is only found on the granitic island of Frégate, although it is likely that it was previously more widespread. It is a large, brown, flightless beetle, and has a round abdomen up to 30mm long, with small, raised bumps on the wing-cases. The beetle is nocturnal and can often be seen in groups on rotting tree trunks, particularly after dark. As it is flightless and slow moving, the beetle has developed defensive glands, which secrete a chemical when it is threatened. Due to its limited geographic range, it is vulnerable to extinction.

Longhorn Beetle *Olenecamptus bilobus* LENGTH 2cm n

INNER ISLANDS Granitic islands. **IUCN** Not Evaluated.

A small attractive beetle with a pale brown body and distinctive orange-and-white markings on the abdomen, the adult has long, segmented antennae. The species is often found in gardens, as well as in forested areas.

Father Filibert's Beetle

Frégate Island Giant Tenebrionid Beetle

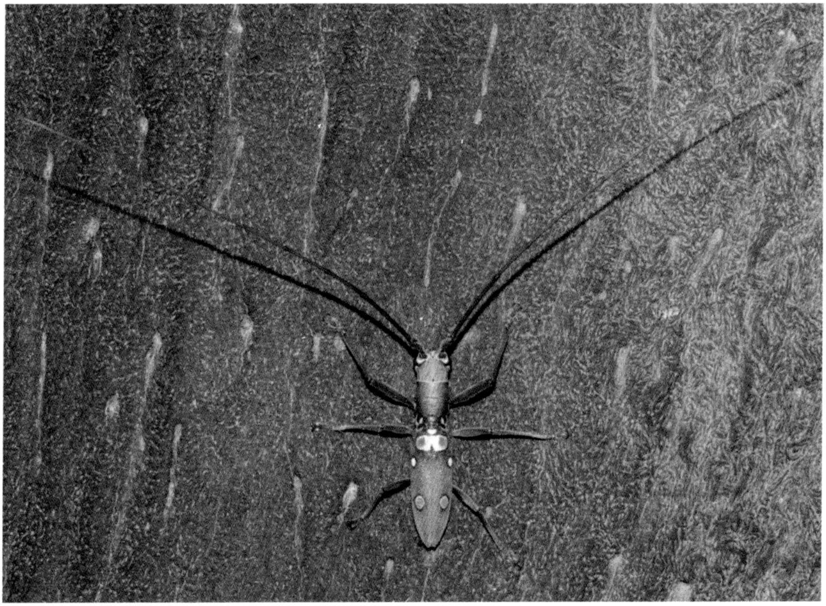

Longhorn Beetle

BUTTERFLIES & MOTHS

Butterflies and moths are contained in the Lepidoptera order, the second largest order of any animal. These insects undergo a complete metamorphosis from an egg to a caterpillar, then a chrysalis, and finally the adult butterfly or moth (imago). Most species feed through a specialized tube known as a proboscis, designed to provide access to the nectar of flowers. In addition to species found in Seychelles year round, the islands also receive many migratory species.

Eggfly *Hypolimnas misippus* **LENGTH** 6cm (n)

(Papiyon)

INNER & OUTER ISLANDS Coralline and granitic islands. **IUCN** Least Concern.
The Eggfly is a relatively common butterfly often seen in gardens on the larger granitic islands during the north-west monsoon. The species is sexually dimorphic, with the male being black with large white spots, while the female is orange and resembles the African Monarch butterfly *Danaus chrysippus*.

African Grass Blue *Zizeeria knysna* **LENGTH** 2cm (i)

(Papiyon ble)

INNER & OUTER ISLANDS Coralline and granitic islands. **IUCN** Least Concern.
The most commonly encountered butterfly in Seychelles, the African Grass Blue is a small species with grey to blue wings in males and brown wings in females. It can be seen flying close to the ground, and feeding on small flowers in gardens and along the sides of roads.

African Death's-head Hawkmoth *Acherontia atropos*

LENGTH 10cm (n)

(Lay)

INNER & OUTER ISLANDS Coralline and granitic islands. **IUCN** Not Evaluated.
The African Death's-head Hawkmoth is a large, widespread moth found in Europe, much of Africa and east to India. The body and wings are brown, often with amber and orange flecks, and there is a characteristic skull-like pattern on the thorax. It is known to produce a squeaking noise.

Wahlberg's Plume Moth *Stenodacma wahlbergi* **LENGTH** 1.5cm (n)

INNER AND OUTER ISLANDS. IUCN Not Evaluated.
Wahlberg's Plume Moth has a beige to orange, 'T'-shaped body with white markings. The wings have a feather-like appearance. It is active at night and rests on vegetation during the day. The species has a short lifespan of approximately 30 days.

Eggfly

African Grass Blue

African Death's-head Hawkmoth

Wahlberg's Plume Moth

BEES & WASPS

Bees, wasps and ants comprise the order Hymenoptera, which is well represented in Seychelles. Some Hymenoptera display 'sociality', where individuals have developed into different castes, becoming dissimilar in appearance according to the roles they play within a colony.

Western Honey Bee *Apis mellifera* LENGTH 1.5cm ⓘ

(Mous dimyel)

INNER & OUTER ISLANDS Coralline and granitic islands. **IUCN** Data Deficient.
This common bee species is present throughout the granitic islands and many of the coralline islands. It occurs in gardens, where it can be seen flying between flowers. Unlike many bee species, Western Honey Bees have colonies that last for several years.

Carpenter Bee *Xylocopa caffra* LENGTH 2cm ⓝ

(Mous brenzel)

INNER & OUTER ISLANDS Aldabra atoll, coralline and granitic islands.
IUCN Least Concern.
A distinctive bee with a large, round body and broad abdomen, the wings and body of the Carpenter Bee are black, often with a double yellow band towards the front of the abdomen. The species prefers large, brightly coloured flowers, and produces a loud buzzing sound when in flight.

Paper Wasp *Polistes olivaceus* LENGTH 2cm ⓝ

(Mous zonn)

INNER & OUTER ISLANDS Coralline and granitic islands. **IUCN** Least Concern.
A large colonial wasp species common throughout the Seychelles, the Paper Wasp occurs in a variety of habitats, including areas close to human habitation. It has a yellow body with pale brown stripes across the abdomen, and is capable of delivering a nasty sting.

Potter Wasp *Delta alluaudi* LENGTH 2.5cm ⓔ

(Mous mason)

INNER ISLANDS Coralline and granitic islands. **IUCN** Least Concern.
This relatively large, black-and-orange wasp, with dark iridescent wings, is endemic to the granitic islands, but has since been introduced to some of the coralline islands. It builds characteristic mud chambers for its grub, often on the sides of buildings and sometimes on walls inside houses.

Western Honey Bee

Carpenter Bee

Paper Wasp

Potter Wasp

 The Purple Cynorkis orchid.

SEYCHELLES FLORA

Although the islands of Seychelles occupy an area of only 455km^2 and are spread across 115 islands in the western Indian Ocean, they support a diverse array of higher flowering plants. To date, more than 1,300 plant species have been recorded in Seychelles, of which almost 370 are native. Furthermore, at least 100 of these species are endemic and found nowhere else on Earth. It is this endemism, a characteristic of island nations, that makes Seychelles flora particularly fascinating.

Seychelles ranks as one of the countries with the highest forest cover, as a percentage of land area. This figure, however, does not tell the full story, as the vegetation of Seychelles has changed remarkably since humans first set foot on the islands. The granitic islands, which are home to the majority of the population, have seen the most significant transformation. The coastal plateaux, which were once dominated by mangroves and native trees, have given way to a mixture of Coconut plantations, wasteland and urban development. At higher altitudes, native species have been marginalized by the introduction of Cinnamon and Cocoplum, and plantations of Tea and Santol have further replaced areas of forest.

Despite the influence of humans, there do remain areas, particularly at the highest altitudes, where native and endemic plant species are found, and in recent decades a change in focus from extractive forestry to rehabilitation has seen areas of native vegetation being restored.

It would not be possible to include all the species of plant recorded in Seychelles in the following pages – and doing so would fall outside the remit of this book. Instead some of the most commonly encountered species are described, including native, endemic and introduced plants, together with species that may hold a particular interest due to their biology or scarcity. Introduced species that are particularly abundant along coastlines and on walking trails have also been included.

COASTAL ZONE

The narrow strip of coastline that makes up the littoral zone plays host to a variety of plant species. Mangroves inhabit the tidal lagoons and bay areas, perfectly adapted to the extreme waterlogged and saline conditions. On the beach crests, native shrubs and trees, themselves capable of withstanding high levels of salinity, help stabilize the islands' shores.

White Mangrove *Avicennia marina* n

(Mangliye blan)

INNER ISLANDS Cousin, Curieuse, La Digue, Mahé, Marianne, Praslin, Silhouette, Thèrese. **OUTER ISLANDS** Aldabra atoll, Astove, Cosmoledo atoll, Farquhar atoll. **IUCN** Least Concern.

The most common of the mangrove species found within the Seychelles Granitic islands, this is a small mangrove tree with grey bark, which grows to 6m in height. It bears pale green fruits and yellow to bright orange, star-shaped flowers. Slender, pencil-like roots emerge from the sand beneath the tree. The species prefers raised intertidal areas on the landward side.

Red Mangrove *Rhizophora mucronata* n

(Mangliye rouz)

INNER ISLANDS Cousin, Curieuse, La Digue, Mahé, Marianne, Praslin, Récif, Silhouette. **OUTER ISLANDS** Aldabra atoll, Amirantes group, Astove, Cosmoledo atoll, Farquhar atoll. **IUCN** Least Concern.

This large, widespread mangrove species grows to 15m tall. Long aerial stilt roots protrude from the central stem, and the large, waxy leaves are dark green and elliptical. The flowers are a creamy-yellow colour. The long, narrow propagules, up to 50cm long, are designed to fall from the tree when ripe, sink into the mud and start growing. The species favours the seaward edge of the intertidal zone.

Oriental Mangrove *Bruguiera gymnorhiza* n

(Mangliye lat)

INNER ISLANDS Curieuse, Mahé, Praslin, Silhouette. **OUTER ISLANDS** Aldabra atoll, Astove, Cosmoledo atoll. **IUCN** Least Concern.

A small mangrove tree that grows to a maximum of 10m in height, the Oriental Mangrove has distinctive knee-like aerial roots that emerge from the surrounding substrate. The trunk becomes buttressed in older individuals. The propagules grow to 15cm long and possess a spiky calyx. The species is associated with intertidal zones, particularly in soft-bottomed areas adjacent to river mouths. The wood of the Oriental Mangrove is waterproof and extremely tough, making it valuable for timber.

White Mangrove

Red Mangrove

Oriental Mangrove

Mangrove Apple *Sonneratia alba* (n)

(Mangliye fler)

INNER ISLANDS Mahé. **OUTER ISLANDS** Aldabra atoll, Cosmoledo atoll, Astove. **IUCN** Least Concern.

A large mangrove species that grows to 15m in height, the Mangrove Apple's finger-like aerial roots are conical and grow to 60cm above the substrate. The leaves are stiff and rounded, while the white flowers, which open at night, are a mass of white stamens. The tree prefers the seaward fringe of the intertidal zone.

Black Mangrove *Lumnitzera racemosa* (n)

(Mangliye pti fey)

INNER ISLANDS Conception, Curieuse, Frégate, La Digue, Mahé, Praslin, Silhouette. **OUTER ISLANDS** Aldabra atoll, Astove. **IUCN** Least Concern.

A small mangrove growing to 5m tall, the Black Mangrove's leaves are small, thick and waxy, with slightly notched edges. The tree bears shiny green bulbous fruits, which are slightly flattened, and small white flowers with five petals. It has knee-like aerial roots, although they are more feathery than those of the Oriental Mangrove (p. 100). The species prefers less saline conditions and is often found on the landward edge of the intertidal zone.

Puzzle Nut Mangrove *Xylocarpus granatum* (n)

(Mangliye ponm)

INNER ISLANDS Curieuse, Mahé. **OUTER ISLANDS** Aldabra atoll, Cosmoledo atoll. **IUCN** Least Concern.

The Puzzle Nut Mangrove is a small tree that grows to 8m in height. It has a complex intertwining buttress root system with plank-like aerial roots. The bark is light brown to yellow and often flaking. It has small, cream to white flowers and irregular seeds, which fit together like a 3D jigsaw, hence the English name. The species favours the landward edge of the intertidal zone.

Beach Morning Glory *Ipomoea* sp. (n)

(Patatran rouz)

INNER & OUTER ISLANDS Most islands. **IUCN** Not Evaluated.

This coastal liana has large, bright purple-pink flowers, which open in the morning and close in the afternoon. The two-lobed leaves are smooth and leathery. A widespread pioneer species, salt tolerant and capable of stabilizing sand, the plant forms a creeping mat over rocks and sand and is common on Seychelles' beaches.

Mangrove Apple

Black Mangrove

Puzzle Nut Mangrove

Beach Morning Glory

Scaevola *Scaevola taccada*

(Vouloutye)

INNER & OUTER ISLANDS Most islands. **IUCN** Not Evaluated.

A common shrub throughout Seychelles, the Scaevola bears large, bright green, glossy leaves with small, white, fan-like flowers. The berry-like fruits turn from green to white and each contains a single seed, which is dispersed in sea water. The species prefers coastal areas, where it forms part of the beach-crest vegetation, and is hardy and salt tolerant.

Coconut *Cocos nucifera* 

(Pye koko)

INNER & OUTER ISLANDS Most islands. **IUCN** Not Evaluated.

This large palm grows to 30m in height. The pinnate leaves radiate from the crown, with the pinnae reaching up to 90cm. Believed by many to be a native species that naturally colonized the coastal fringes of islands, it is now very common on almost all the islands, where it was once planted extensively in plantations to produce copra, with exotic varieties of coconut often being used to boost production. Coconut plantations remain in many areas.

Alexandrian Laurel *Calophyllum inophyllum*

(Takamaka)

INNER ISLANDS Most granitic islands. **OUTER ISLANDS** Most islands.
IUCN Least Concern.

The Alexandrian Laurel is a large, slow-growing tree with very hard wood and fissured bark. The leaves are dark green and glossy, while the small white flowers contain yellow stamens. It is often found on beaches, where it has been planted to stop coastal erosion. The timber is valued for the production of furniture.

Fish Poison Tree *Barringtonia asiatica*

(Bonnen kare)

INNER ISLANDS Most granitic islands. **OUTER ISLANDS** Most Amirantes islands, Coëtivy, Denis. **IUCN** Least Concern.

This large tree has long, shiny leaves and short leaf stems that form part of a dense canopy. The flowers are large with numerous stamens that are white at the base, becoming pink towards the tips. They open in the evening, producing a sickly sweet smell, and fall to the ground in the morning. The fruits are box-like in appearance and are able to float. When crushed, the leaves produce a poison and in some parts of the world this is used to stun fish.

Scaevola

Coconut

Alexandrian Laurel

Fish Poison Tree

Sea Hibiscus *Hibiscus tiliaceus* n

(Var)

INNER & OUTER ISLANDS Most islands. **IUCN** Least Concern.

A common coastal tree, the Sea Hibiscus is found on beaches and near mangroves, where it is adapted to tolerate elevated salt levels. It grows to a height of 10m and has heart-shaped leaves. The yellow flowers turn orange, then red, over the course of a day before they fall.

Jackbean *Canavalia cathartica* n

(Pwamaron)

INNER ISLANDS Aride, Bird, Cerf, Cousin, Curieuse, Denis, Felicité, Frégate, Mahé, North Island, Praslin, Solhouette, Ste Anne. **OUTER ISLANDS** Aldabra, Coëtivy, Cosmoledo, D'Arros, Poivre. **IUCN** Not Evaluated.

This vigorous climber is found on beach crests and the coastal plateaux, often covering other plant species. Each leaf has three rounded leaflets, and the bright pink flowers hang in clusters.

Casuarina *Casuarina equisetifolia* i

(Sed)

INNER & OUTER ISLANDS Most islands. **IUCN** Least Concern.

A conifer-like tree with numerous jointed green stems, the Casuarina grows to 20m in height and is common along coastlines, but can also be found in mountain areas. It produces small, dry fruiting structures, which frequently litter the floor at the base of the tree.

COASTAL PLATEAUX & LOW-ALTITUDE FORESTS

The coastal plateaux of the granitic islands consist of woodland comprising both native and introduced species. Wetlands are found on many of the islands, although development has reduced the area they cover. Similarly, the low-altitude forests that once covered extensive areas of the plateaux have been much reduced in size.

Indian Almond *Terminalia catappa* n

(Badamier, Bodanmyen)

INNER & OUTER ISLANDS Most islands. **IUCN** Least Concern.

The Indian Almond is a tall tree with a straight trunk and horizontal branches that form multiple layers. It is deciduous, with the large, glossy leaves turning yellow, orange and red before they fall to the ground. Is found in a variety of habitats, from the coast to mid altitudes.

Sea Hibiscus

Jackbean

Casuarina

Indian Almond

Giant-leaved Fig *Ficus lutea* n

(Lafous gran fey)

INNER & OUTER ISLANDS Most islands. **IUCN** Least Concern.

A large fig tree with elliptic to oblong green leaves and small yellow fruits, the Giant-leave Fig is capable of growing to 25m in height, although it is usually shorter. The figs cluster towards the end of the branchlets, where they fruit directly from the stem.

Pisonia *Pisonia grandis* n

(Mapou)

INNER ISLANDS Aride, Cousin, Cousine, Frégate, Mamelles, Récif. **OUTER ISLANDS** Most islands. **IUCN** Not Evaluated.

A relatively tall flowering tree with smooth bark and thin leaves, this species is common on seabird islands. The seeds of Pisonia stick to birds' feathers and are spread between islands. On occasion, a bird will become overloaded with fruits to the point of being unable to fly.

Elephant Ear *Alocasia macrorrhiza* i

(Vya)

INNER & OUTER ISLANDS Inhabited islands. **IUCN** Not Evaluated.

The Elephant Ear is an easily identifiable, widespread plant with large, glossy leaves on rigid stalks. The leaves stand upright, pointing skywards. The species was introduced and is now present on most of the larger granitic islands, as well as several coralline islands.

Indian Mulberry *Morinda citrifolia* n

(Bwa torti)

INNER & OUTER ISLANDS Most islands. **IUCN** Not Evaluated.

The Indian Mulberry, or Noni, is a small, fruit-bearing shrub common on the granitic islands, where it is found in a range of habitats from the coast to exposed glacis. The plant produces a fruit that turns yellow, then white as it ripens, emitting a pungent odour in the process.

Wright's Gardenia *Rothmannia annae* e

(Bwa sitron)

INNER ISLANDS Aride. **IUCN** Critically Endangered.

Although it is cultivated in some gardens and has been reintroduced to other islands, the only remaining truly wild population of Wright's Gardenia is restricted to the island of Aride. This small tree produces beautiful white-and-purple flowers, which give out a wonderful scent.

Giant-leaved Fig

Pisonia

Elephant Ear

Indian Mulberry

Wright's Gardenia

GARDENS, PARKS & ROADSIDES

On the larger, inhabited granitic islands, parks, gardens and roadsides are dominated by introduced and ornamental species, while many of the coralline islands have remnant Coconut plantations. Fruit trees including banana and Papaya are found alongside varieties of hibiscus and frangipani.

Madagascar Periwinkle *Catharanthus roseus*

(Roz anmer)

INNER & OUTER ISLANDS Most islands. **IUCN** Not Evaluated.

The Madagascar Periwinkle is an attractive widespread herbaceous plant with oval leaves that bears white to bright pink flowers with dark red centres. The plant has long been used as a herbal medicine, and its alkaloids have been extracted for use in the treatment of leukaemia.

Bougainvillea *Bougainvillea glabra*

(Vilea)

INNER & OUTER ISLANDS Inhabited islands. **IUCN** Least Concern.

This popular ornamental plant is common in gardens. Its modified leaves (bracts) occur in a wide range of spectacular colours, while the small flowers are white. A climbing plant with a thick, thorny stem, it prefers soil with good drainage.

Blue Trumpet Vine *Thunbergia grandiflora*

(Lalyann tronpet)

INNER ISLANDS La Digue, Mahé, Praslin. **IUCN** Not Evaluated.

An introduced plant, the Blue Trumpet Vine is common on the three most populated granitic islands. It is a vigorous climber, capable of growing to 15m and covering native vegetation. It bears large, triangular leaves and attractive trumpet-shaped flowers varying in colour from white to blue and lilac.

Passion Flower *Passiflora edulis*

(Frilapasyon)

INNER ISLANDS Frégate, La Digue, Mahé, Praslin, Silhouette. **IUCN** Not Evaluated.

Originally from South America, the Passion Flower is common on the larger granitic islands, where it is both cultivated and widespread in woodland and areas of scrubland. It is a climbing plant with distinctive white flowers and spherical fruits, which are said to attract rats.

Madagascar Periwinkle

Bougainvillea

Blue Trumpet Vine

Passion Flower

Hibiscus *Hibiscus* spp.

(Ibiskis)

INNER ISLANDS Bird, Curieuse, Denis, Frégate, La Digue, Mahé, Praslin, Silhouette. **OUTER ISLANDS** Amirantes. **IUCN** NA.

Several varieties of hibiscus, including hybrids, are to be found in Seychelles, where they are common in gardens and along roadside hedges. They are particularly popular with hotels and guest houses, and occur in a variety of colours, of which red is the most common.

Frangipani *Plumeria rubra, P. obtusa*

(Franzipan)

INNER & OUTER ISLANDS Inhabited islands. **IUCN** Least Concern.

Both species of frangipani are native to Central America, but they are common in gardens and along roadsides throughout Seychelles inner islands. The flowers of *P. rubra* occur in a variety of colours, while those of *P. obtusa* are always white with a white centre. Often used in decorations, the flowers are highly scented.

Bilimbi *Averrhoa bilimbi*

(Bilenbi)

INNER ISLANDS Most islands. **OUTER ISLANDS** Alphonse, Coëtivy, Desroches, Farquahar, Marie Louise, Platte, Poivre. **IUCN** Not Evaluated.

A cultivated tropical tree, the Bilimbi grows to 8m in height. The pinnate leaves contain numerous leaflets, while the small flowers are red to purple. The fruits are bright green, elongated berries with a sour taste. Bilimbi is one of the preferred fruits of the Seychelles Black Parrot (p. 24).

Starfruit *Averrhoa carambola*

(Karanbol)

INNER ISLANDS Cerf Island, Frégate, La Digue, Mahé, Praslin, Silhouette. **IUCN** Data Deficient.

This commonly cultivated fruit tree is found in gardens on the larger granitic islands. The waxy fruit, which is star shaped in cross-section, is orange when ripe. The trees are densely branched and produce small, white-and-purple flowers.

Papaya *Carica papaya*

(Papay)

INNER & OUTER ISLANDS Most islands. **IUCN** Not Evaluated.

This introduced species is valued for its fruits, which are eaten raw when ripe or cooked when green. The tree-like plant is thick stemmed and contains obvious scarring, while the deeply lobed leaves form the crown. Female trees have larger flowers than male trees, and produce the fruits.

Hibiscus

Frangipani

Bilimbi

Starfruit

Papaya

Banana *Musa* spp.

(Pye bannan)

INNER ISLANDS Granitic islands. **OUTER ISLANDS** Some low-lying coralline islands. **IUCN** Not Evaluated.

There are numerous varieties of this large cultivated herb in Seychelles. The large green leaves reach 2.5m in length and become torn with age. Banana plants are usually chopped down after they have fruited, with new 'trees' propagated through shoots from the rhizomes.

Cassava *Manihot esculenta*

(Mayok)

INNER ISLANDS Granitic islands. **IUCN** Not Evaluated.

This introduced species, native to South America, is widely cultivated and common in gardens. The leaves are deeply lobed, while the stems are reddish in colour. The edible starch-rich roots grow to 80cm in length and are white to yellow in colour. Both the leaves and the roots contain toxins and should not be consumed raw.

Mango *Mangifera indica*

(Mang)

INNER ISLANDS Most granitic islands. **IUCN** Data Deficient.

The mango is a popular cultivated fruit found throughout the larger granitic islands. Mango trees can grow to 40m in height and have a dense crown of long, narrow leaves. The fruits occur in numerous sizes and tend to be oval or kidney shaped. Globally there are more than 200 varieties of mango and several varieties are found in Seychelles. When ripe, the orange flesh is juicy and sweet.

Breadfruit *Artocarpus altilis*

(Friyapen)

INNER ISLANDS Granitic islands. **OUTER ISLANDS** Many low-lying coralline islands. **IUCN** Not Evaluated.

A large tree, which grows to 20m, the Breadfruit is common in gardens. The dark green, glossy leaves are distinctively lobed, while the green fruits are spherical and produce a milk-like juice. They can weigh nearly 2kg and measure 20cm in diameter. Rich in starch, breadfruit is commonly baked, boiled or fried as chips.

Banana

Cassava

Mango

Breadfruit

MID- & HIGH-ALTITUDE FORESTS

The mid-altitude forests of the larger granitic islands are dominated by species such as Cinnamon. Below the canopy, native ferns and endemic palms compete for space with introduced species. At higher altitudes, pockets of endemic trees are still found in places, along with screwpines in more exposed areas.

Bird's Nest Fern *Asplenium nidus* n

(Lang de bef)

INNER ISLANDS La Digue, Mahé, Praslin, Silhouette. **OUTER ISLANDS** Alphonse. **IUCN** Not Evaluated.

An epiphytic fern found predominantly on the larger islands, the large smooth, glossy fronds of the Bird's Nest Fern radiate from a nest-like clump. It favours mid- to high-altitude forests, where it can be found growing from the trunks and branches of trees.

Seychelles Tree Fern *Cyathea sechellarum* e

(Fanzon)

INNER ISLANDS Mahé, Silhouette. **IUCN** Not Evaluated.

The only endemic tree fern found in Seychelles, the Seychelles Tree Fern grows to a height of 10m. Large, divided fronds radiate from a tall, slender stem. It favours high-altitude forests with moist conditions.

King Fern *Angiopteris madagascariensis* n

(Baton monsennyer)

INNER ISLANDS Mahé, Silhouette. **IUCN** Not Evaluated.

The fronds of this large fern grow to more than 3m in length. They are dark green and waxy, and are divided into large pinnae. The species is similar to the less common *A. chongsengiana*, and is often found alongside streams in mid-altitude forests.

Wart Fern *Phymatosorus scolopendria* n

(Kapiler)

INNER & OUTER ISLANDS Several islands. **IUCN** Not Evaluated.

This common fern species has large, glossy, lobe-shaped fronds. The undersides of the fronds are covered in distinctive sporangia, which appear like warts on the upperside. The fronds extend from a creeping rhizome, which grows over rocks, trees and the ground.

Spikemoss *Selaginella sechellarum* e

(Lapat lezar)

INNER ISLANDS Mahé, Praslin, Silhouette. **IUCN** Not Evaluated.

A small, fern-like plant that grows close to the forest floor, the Spikemoss prefers moist conditions at mid altitudes. The Creole name 'Lapat leza' refers to the fact that the ends of the creeping stems look like the feet of geckos.

Bird's Nest Fern

Seychelles Tree Fern

King Fern

Wart Fern

Spikemoss

Koster's Curse *Clidemia hirta*

(Fowatouk)

INNER ISLANDS Mahé, North Island, Silhouette. **IUCN** Not Evaluated.

An introduced weed-like shrub, Koster's Curse appears to be spreading on Mahé and Silhouette Islands. The 12cm-long leaves are covered in small hairs and the purple fruit is edible. The shrub can cover large areas of the forest floor, particularly in open areas.

Vanilla *Vanilla planifolia*

(Lavannir)

INNER ISLANDS Curieuse, Denis, La Digue, Mahé, Praslin, Silhouette.
IUCN Least Concern.

Once an important component of the economy, vanilla production has virtually ceased apart from on a plantation on La Digue. Vanilla plants have since spread into forest habitats, but they do not produce seedpods due to a lack of natural pollinators. The plant is easily distinguishable from the endemic vanilla species, due to the presence of leaves along the stem.

Cinnamon *Cinnamomum verum*

(Kanel)

INNER ISLANDS Most granitic islands. **IUCN** Not Evaluated.

One of the most abundant trees on the granitic islands, Cinnamon was deliberately planted for the production of leaf oil in the early twentieth century. The tree grows to 17m in height and has a distinctive aromatic bark, which is still cropped on a small scale. The green leaves are red when young and have three prominent veins.

White Albizzia *Falcataria moluccana*

(Albizya)

INNER ISLANDS Most granitic islands. **IUCN** Not Evaluated.

A quick-growing, introduced species, originally from southeast Asia, this tree is common at mid to high altitudes, where it grows to 35m in height, with a recognizable umbrella-shaped crown. It often outcompetes native trees by drawing huge amounts of water from streams and small rivers. It flowers at certain times of the year, producing yellow-white, scented flowers.

Koster's Curse

Vanilla

Cinnamon

White Albizzia

Jackfruit *Artocarpus heterophyllus* (i)

(Zak)

INNER ISLANDS Most granitic islands. **IUCN** Not Evaluated.

A common cultivated tree, the Jackfruit grows to 15m in height. Originally from India and Southeast Asia, it is part of the breadruit family. It produces characteristic edible fruits with a yellow warty exterior and a pungent odour. Individual fruits can weigh more than 30kg and mature trees can provide over 200 fruits in one year. The tree has a smooth red-to-brown bark, which releases a milky sap if cut. The species favours mid- to high-altitude forests and is afforded protected status in Seychelles.

Coco Marron *Curculigo seychellensis* (e)

(Koko Maron)

INNER ISLANDS Curieuse, Félicité, Mahé, Praslin, Silhouette, Therese. **IUCN** Least Concern.

An endemic terrestrial herb with upright leaf stems covered in black thorns, the Coco Marron grows to 2m in height and produces cream to yellow flowers, which cluster at the base of the plant. It is associated with a number of habitats, including glacis and forests at mid to high altitudes.

Dillenia *Dillenia ferruginea* (e)

(Bwa rouz)

INNER ISLANDS Curieuse, Mahé, Praslin, Silhouette. **IUCN** Near Threatened.

An endemic tree, the Dillenia grows to a height of 20m. It is found on four of the granitic islands, where it prefers woodland at mid to high altitudes. The leaves are thick and ridged, often with numerous holes, while the small white flowers develop into orange fleshy fruits.

Northia *Northia seychellana* (e)

(Kapisen)

INNER ISLANDS Curieuse, Mahé, Praslin, Silhouette. **IUCN** Not Evaluated.

The Northia is a distinctive endemic tree found at mid to high altitudes. The lanceolate leaves are dark green on the upperside and red to brown underneath. They cluster at the ends of the branches, which contain numerous bumps. The tree can grow to 20m in height, but is often much smaller and shrub-like. The ripe fruit is brown and 10cm in diameter.

Jackfruit

Coco Marron

Dillenia

Northia

Coco-de-mer *Lodoicea maldivica* ⓔ

(Kokodmer)

INNER ISLANDS Curieuse, Praslin (planted on other islands). **IUCN** Endangered.
The mythical Coco-de-mer is perhaps the most famous of all Seychelles' flora. The name means 'coco of the sea' in English and Creole, and is derived from a belief that the trees grow under the sea. This myth dates back to a time before the discovery of Seychelles, when the palm was only known from nuts that had washed ashore in the Maldives and Sri Lanka.

The palm is found on Praslin and neighbouring Curieuse Island. In the Vallée de Mai and Fond Ferdinand on Praslin, it is the dominant species and supports a variety of native wildlife. The plants are either male or female, and the palms can reach 35m in height, but are slow growing, with females taking 25 years before they can bear fruits. Mature female plants may have many fruits, with each taking up to seven years to mature. The fruit is large and olive coloured, and holds the record for being the heaviest in the world. It encloses a bi-lobed seed, which can weigh up to 18kg and is the largest seed in the world.

Due to the male inflorescences and the female nut resembling human sexual body parts, the Coco-de-mer has achieved legendary status, while the kernel is considered an aphrodisiac in Southeast Asia. The Seychelles government exercises strict control over the collection of nuts, and a limited number of processed nuts is sold, with individual identification numbers to verify their legality. Despite this, poaching for the black market continues to represent a threat to the species.

Palmiste *Deckenia nobilis* ⓔ

(Palmis)

INNER ISLANDS Concéption, Curieuse, Félicité, La Digue, Mahé, Praslin, Silhouette, North Island, Thèrese. **IUCN** Vulnerable.
This tall, slender palm grows to more than 35m in height. The unbranched trunk gives way to a crown consisting of very large (up to 5m long), feathery leaves. Young plants and seedlings have yellow spines at the bases of the stems. The flowering bodies of the palm are protected by a spiny purse, which drops to the ground as they mature. Palmiste was traditionally harvested for the palm hearts at the growing tip and used in Millionaire Salad, or Palm Heart Salad. The removal of this growing tip kills the palm, making it susceptible to overexploitation. Today, the palm is protected by law and the growing tips of the Coconut have replaced those of Palmiste in most salads.

Coco-de-mer

Palmiste

Millipede Palm *Nephrosperma vanhoutteanum* **e**

(Latannyen milpat)

INNER ISLANDS Cerf, Concéption, Curieuse, Frégate, Mahé, Praslin, Silhouette, St Anne, Thèrese. **IUCN** Least Concern.

This slender palm can grow to 14m in height, although it is usually shorter. The terminal crown has several large pinnate leaves, and inflorescences up to 2.5m long consisting of numerous small, male and female yellow flowers. The leaf stems tend to be red in younger plants and have black spines. The species is found in a variety of habitats, from exposed glacis to forests at low to mid altitudes.

Thief Palm *Phoenicophorium borsigianum* **e**

(Latannyen fey)

INNER ISLANDS Cerf, Concéption, Curieuse, Felicité, Frégate, La Digue, Mahé, Praslin, Silhouette, St Anne, Thèrese. **IUCN** Least Concern.

This common endemic palm can grow to 15m in height. It has very large leaves (to 2m long), which are split at the ends. Younger plants often have undivided leaves with orange borders, and leaf stems covered in black spikes. The inflorescences are similar to those in the Millipede Palm (above). A drought-tolerant species, the Thief Palm occurs in exposed areas, as well as in low- to mid-altitude forests. The leaves have traditionally been used in thatching.

Latanier Palm *Roscheria melanochaetes* **e**

(Latannyen oban)

INNER ISLANDS Frégate, Mahé, Praslin, Silhouette. **IUCN** Near Threatened.

The smallest of Seychelles' endemic palms, the Latanier Palm grows to 8m in height. The young leaves are red, while the mature green leaves are large (2.5m long) and divided into irregular, broad leaflets. The narrow trunk has small stilt roots and is covered in numerous black spines. The species prefers damp habitats and shaded forests at mid to high altitudes, where it is often found in the understorey.

Stilt Palm *Verschaffeltia splendida* **e**

(Latannyen lat)

INNER ISLANDS Felicité, Frégate, St Anne, Mahé, Praslin, Slihouette.
IUCN Near Threatened.

This tall endemic palm grows to a height of 30m. It has large, rounded leaves with a 'V'-shaped split at the tip. The mature leaves often become shredded by the wind. Young plants have black spines on the leaf stems. The species prefers damp habitats in mid- to high-altitude forests, and frequently borders mountain streams.

Millipede Palm

Thief Palm

Latanier Palm

Stilt Palm

Horne's Pandanus *Martellidendron hornei* e

(Vakwa Parasol)

INNER ISLANDS Curieuse, Frégate, La Digue, Mahé, Praslin, Silhouette.

IUCN Vulnerable.

A tall species of screwpine, Horne's Pandanus grows to a height of more than 15m. Multiple aerial roots at the base give way to a tall trunk with a distinctive parasol-shaped crown. The tree produces large green fruiting bodies, which are orange inside when ripe. It prefers damp areas in mid- to high-altitude environments, often next to water sources.

GLACIS & SCRUBLAND

The exposed granite rocks known as glacis are found from sea level to high altitudes throughout Seychelles' inner granitic island group, and support a variety of native and endemic plant species. Both here and on the raised coral rock of the Aldabra group, plant species are specifically adapted to survive in challenging environments with nutrient-poor soils.

Seychelles Pandanus *Pandanus sechellarum* e

(Vakwa maron)

INNER ISLANDS Curieuse, Felicité, Frégate, La Digue, Mahé, Praslin, Silhouette.

IUCN Near Threatened.

This large endemic screwpine grows to 15m in height. The aerial roots are stout and widely spaced, often emerging from immediately below the crown. The slender green leaves have prickly pink spines along the margins. The species prefers exposed glacis and open wet forests.

Balfour's Pandanus *Pandanus balfourii* n

(Vakwa bordmer)

INNER ISLANDS Most granitic islands. **IUCN** Vulnerable.

Balfour's Pandanus is the most widespread species on Seychelles' granitic islands, growing to a height of 8m. The trunk branches a couple of metres above the ground and occasionally has small aerial roots at the base. The slender green leaves have prickly white spines along the margins. The species favours coastal areas, including glacis and shorelines.

Mountain Pandanus *Pandanus multispicatus* e

(Vakwa montany)

INNER ISLANDS Conception, Curieuse, Felicité, Frégate, La Digue, Mahé, Praslin, Silhouette, Thèrese. **IUCN** Near Threatened.

The smallest of the endemic screwpines, the Mountain Pandanus grows to 3m in height. It forms small bushes with narrow, pointed leaves and prickly marginal spines. The small, upright fruiting bodies are often yellow to orange. The species occurs in exposed areas of open glacis, where it is common.

Horne's Pandanus

Seychelles Pandanus

Balfour's Pandanus

Mountain Pandanus

Cocoplum *Chrysobalanus icaco* ⓘ

(Prin de frans)

INNER ISLANDS Most granitic islands. **IUCN** Not Evaluated.

The Cocoplum is common throughout the granitic islands, where it has been planted to prevent soil erosion. It forms dense, bush-like scrub that can be difficult to penetrate. The plant has thick, waxy leaves and produces spherical fruits similar in appearance to small plums.

Jellyfish Tree *Medusagyne oppositifolia* ⓔ

(Bwa mediz)

INNER ISLANDS Mahé. **IUCN** Critically Endangered.

The Jellyfish Tree is a small, Critically Endangered tree confined to Mahé, where only a few dozen trees remain. Growing to 10m in height, the Jellyfish Tree has a dense crown of glossy green leaves and small white flowers. It produces small, oval fruits, which dry out when ripe to release their seeds. When doing so, they resemble parasols or jellyfish, giving the tree its name.

Pineapple *Ananas comosus* ⓘ

(Zannanan)

INNER ISLANDS Granitic islands. **IUCN** Not Evaluated.

Originally from South America, the Pineapple is now cultivated as a crop plant throughout the tropics. The thick stem is surrounded by numerous long, waxy leaves with sharp margins, and the fruit develops in the centre of the plant. Although grown locally, pineapples are not produced in sufficient numbers and many of the fruits available for purchase are imported.

Purple Cynorkis *Cynorkis fastigiata* ⓝ

(Orkid levantay)

INNER ISLANDS Mahé, Praslin, Silhouette, Curieuse, Felicité, Therese.

IUCN Data Deficient.

This small but common orchid favours red-earth soils and grassy areas in forests and mountain clearings. It is a ground orchid with one or two long, slender leaves at its base. A leafless stem gives rise to a pale cream flower with a purple hue on the lateral sepals.

Pigeon Orchid *Dendrobium crumenatum* ⓘ

(Orkid pizon)

INNER ISLANDS Mahé. **IUCN** Data Deficient.

The Pigeon Orchid has long flower stems that become swollen at the base following heavy rain. The stems bear numerous small white flowers with a yellow tongue, which are said to resemble pigeons in flight. Flowering occurs 10 days after a sudden drop in temperature and only lasts for 24 hours.

Cocoplum

Jellyfish Tree

Pineapple

Purple Cynorkis

Pigeon Orchid

Tropicbird Orchid *Angraecum eburneum* n

(Orkid payanke)

INNER ISLANDS Mahé, Praslin, Silhouette. **OUTER ISLANDS** Aldabra atoll. **IUCN** Not Evaluated.

An epiphytic orchid with white flowers, each with a slender green spur, the Tropicbird Orchid is the national flower of Seychelles and is found in open, rocky habitats in forests and on glacis. It is often illegally collected for cultivation in gardens and for use in bridal bouquets.

Wild Vanilla *Vanilla phalaenopsis* e

(Lavannir maron)

INNER ISLANDS Félicité, Mahé, Praslin, Silhouette. **IUCN** Least Concern.

The Wild Vanilla is a climbing, epiphytic orchid with a thick, yellow-green, leafless stem. The white flowers grow to 8cm and have a peach-coloured centre. The fruits are cylindrical capsules that turn from green to black when ripe; they lack the vanillin of cultivated varieties.

Seychelles Pitcher Plant *Nepenthes pervillei* e

(Lalyann potao)

INNER ISLANDS Mahé, Silhouette. **IUCN** Least Concern.

This endemic liana is found on red-earth soil and rocky glacis. It is often associated with bracken ferns. The tendrils provide support to the pitchers and stems, which can reach several metres in length. The pitchers can be 15cm long and contain nectar-producing organs used to attract insects. Once inside them, insects struggle to escape but slip into the liquid at the base of the plant, where they are dissolved by digestive enzymes.

Dianella Lily *Dianella ensifolia* n

(Mangasav)

INNER ISLANDS Mahé, Thérèse. **IUCN** Not Evaluated.

A grass-like herb, the Dianella Lily forms dense clumps to 1.5m high. The long, straight leaves are smooth and contain a central rib. The small attractive flowers are lavender-blue and contain six bright yellow stamens, while the berries are dark blue.

Aldabra Lily *Aloe aldabrensis* e

INNER ISLANDS Aldabra atoll. **IUCN** Not Evaluated.

This aloe species is endemic to Aldabra atoll. It is often solitary, growing close to the ground. It forms a rosette of stiff, green, upright leaves, and produces orange flowers and red to purple berries that are a popular food choice of the Comoros Blue Pigeon (p. 22).

Tropicbird Orchid

Seychelles Pitcher Plant

Dianella Lily

Aldabra Lily

 A trail within the Vallée de Mai, Praslin Island.

NATURE WALKS & HIKING TRAILS

While Seychelles is famed for its pristine beaches and turquoise waters, the islands also offer fantastic hiking opportunities for those wishing to spend some time immersed in nature. The granitic islands are densely forested, with numerous trails accessible throughout the year. With a variety of hiking options for people of all abilities, there really is something for everyone.

Many of the nature trails fall within national parks and are managed by the Seychelles Parks and Gardens Authority (SPGA). Some have an entrance fee, which must be paid before beginning your hike. The SPGA undertakes regular maintenance of the most popular trails, as well as conducting research into the islands' flora and fauna. Invasive species removal and the reintroduction of native and endemic species also serve to protect the nation's biodiversity. For more information about the national parks and entry fees, visit the SPGA website at www.snpa.gov.sc.

Many of the trails included in this book can be enjoyed without the need for a guide. However, professional guides are available and can certainly add to the experience with their local knowledge and expertise. Ask at your hotel or guest house for information on how to book a guide, and never accept offers from unregistered guides.

It is always best to travel light when you are heading on a hike, particularly as the weather can be very hot and humid in the forests. Nevertheless, there are certain items that you should take on every excursion, while others may prove to be useful for specific trails. Regardless of the length of the hike you plan to make, always carry drinking water with you. It is easy to quickly become dehydrated and it is essential that you drink sufficient amounts of water. Likewise, a hat provides necessary protection from the sun. While some trails are predominantly in the open, even forested trails are likely to pass through open areas. To avoid the heat in the middle of the day, it is advisable to begin hiking in the early morning; this also provides the best opportunity for clear views from the various observation platforms, before the clouds begin to gather in the afternoons. If you head out in the afternoon, give yourself plenty of time to return before dark.

In general, hiking in Seychelles is safe and reports of theft are rare. However, you should never hike alone, and it is recommended that you inform your hotel or guest house where you are going and what time you plan to return. There are no large predatory animals or venomous snakes on the islands, and few biting or stinging insects. Take care to avoid Giant Centipedes and Paper Wasps, and make sure you apply mosquito repellent if walking near marsh areas, as there have been cases of dengue fever in recent years.

Some trails are better maintained than others, and a good pair of walking shoes is recommended for all routes. In the rainy season, the ground can become very soft underfoot and a shoe with a good grip that supports the ankle is ideal. It is also worthwhile taking a mobile phone. While not all trails receive a mobile signal, should you find yourself lost you may be able to reach an area where you have reception. Make sure you stay on existing footpaths and follow signs or markings on rocks.

The starting point for most hiking trails on the main islands can be reached by bus or car. If driving by car, make sure not to leave any valuables on display.

The key below provides symbols for some of the items that you may wish to take with you, and the relevant symbols are included on each of the individual hiking pages.

Do not smoke while in the forest, as fires are easily started. Large expanses of forest on Praslin, Ste Anne and other islands have been destroyed by accidental fire. Remember to take any litter back with you, disposing of it properly in a refuse bin. Do not disturb local wildlife, or take any souvenirs. Note that it is illegal to remove any living thing from a national park. As the old saying goes, 'Take only pictures and leave only footprints.'

KEY TO HIKING SYMBOLS

Hiking shoes

Hat

Water

Backpack

Packed lunch

Swimming things

KEY TO MAP SYMBOLS

Hut

Viewpoint

Refreshments

Toilets

Parking

Mountain

Hiking route

MAHÉ ISLAND

Mahé is the largest of the granitic islands and is home to the tallest peak in Seychelles, Morne Seychellois, which stands at 905m. The peak is located within the Morne Seychellois National Park, a protected area that covers more than 30km^2. There are dozens of hiking trails to be found on the island, and there are excellent opportunities to see many endemic species of Seychelles. Mahé is home to seven of the 12 endemic land birds found on the granitic islands, some of which are easily seen along roadsides and in gardens. Others are more elusive and require considerable effort to track down. The Seychelles Scops-owl is perhaps the most difficult to see, remaining active after dark and preferring the forest habitat of the Morne Seychellois National Park. Sadly, the Seychelles White-eye has declined in numbers and only a few birds now remain in the area above Cascade. There are Seychelles White-eye populations on Cousine, Frégate and North Island, but these islands contain upmarket tourist establishments and day visits are not possible.

The forest of the Morne Seychellois National Park is also an excellent place to search for Sooglosid frogs, which are often heard but rarely seen. Gardiner's Pygmy Frog is by far the most common, and inhabits the leaf litter, or is sometimes found on endemic palms. It is not unusual to encounter tree frogs or the Seychelles Wolf Snake, particularly close to streams.

Away from the mid-altitude forests, remnant pockets of mangroves are located at Port Launay and Barbarons. Herons can often be seen hunting for fish, while the mangroves are home to a variety of crab species. On the east coast of Mahé, mangrove forests have developed in the quiet waters between Mahé and the reclamation zone.

Mahé is blessed with numerous outstanding beaches, and despite the rapid rate of development there remain several undisturbed stretches of coastline, particularly in the south of the island. Between September and March, Hawksbill Turtles nest on the southern beaches, with the best time for encounters being during November and December. The beaches and tidal flats also provide feeding grounds for a variety of wading birds, particularly on the east coast.

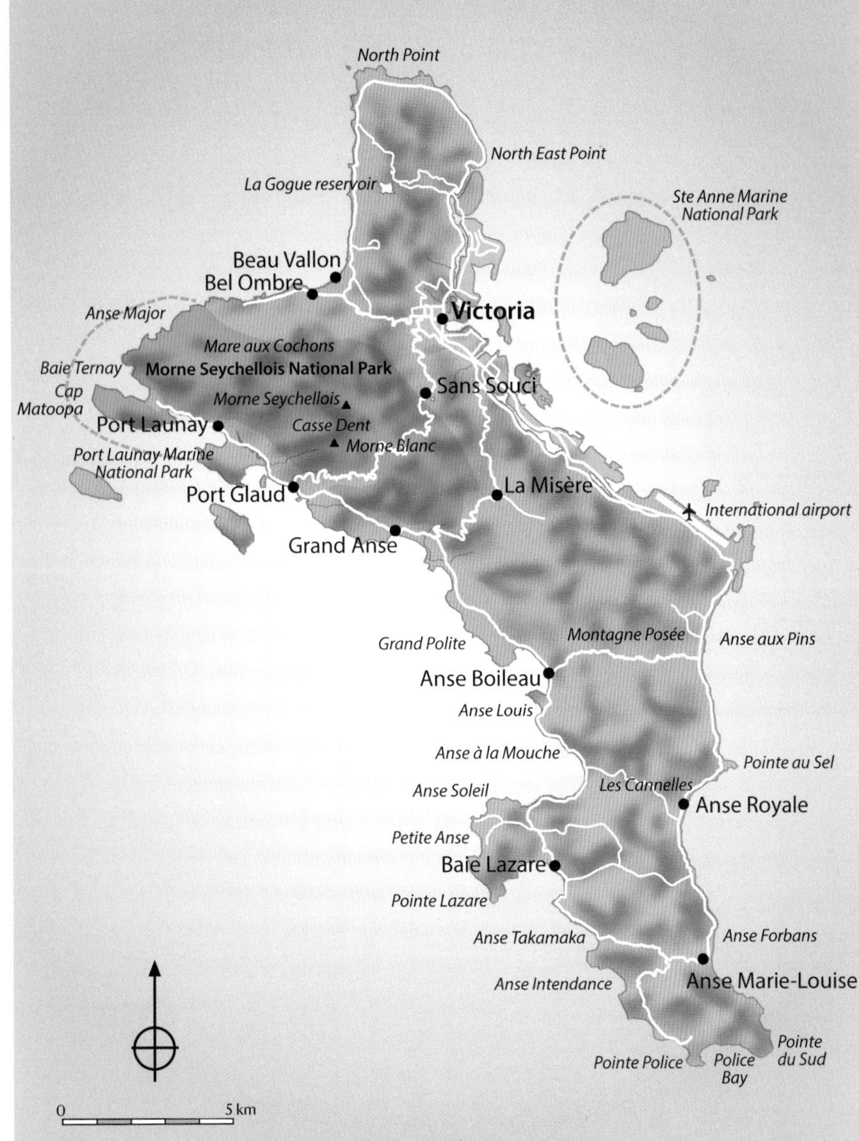
INDIAN OCEAN
North Point
North East Point
La Gogue reservoir
Ste Anne Marine National Park
Beau Vallon
Bel Ombre
Victoria
Anse Major
Mare aux Cochons
Morne Seychellois National Park
Baie Ternay
Cap Matoopa
Sans Souci
Morne Seychellois
Port Launay
Casse Dent
Morne Blanc
Port Launay Marine National Park
Port Glaud
La Misère
International airport
Grand Anse
Grand Polite
Montagne Posée
Anse aux Pins
Anse Boileau
Anse Louis
Anse à la Mouche
Pointe au Sel
Anse Soleil
Les Cannelles
Anse Royale
Petite Anse
Baie Lazare
Pointe Lazare
Anse Takamaka
Anse Forbans
Anse Intendance
Anse Marie-Louise
Pointe Police
Police Bay
Pointe du Sud
0
5 km

Anse Major trail

COASTAL PATH WITH STUNNING VIEWS

Level Beginner
Distance 4km (return trip)
Time 1 hour 20 minutes
Getting there By bus from Victoria bus terminal, Bel Ombre bus stop, or by car but parking might be difficult.

The start of the Anse Major trail begins about 800m after the Bel Ombre bus stop. After getting off the bus opposite the La Scala restaurant, walk up the hill to your left until you reach an exposed glacis with a large property on your left (if driving, there is space for a couple of cars to park here). Continue along the road for another two minutes, passing a drinking fountain on your right (where you can take some water), and you will see the start of the trail on your left-hand side.

The narrow trail cuts its way through the glacis along the coast, with the Morne Seychellois National Park on your left and uninterrupted views of the Indian Ocean to your right, as the glacis slopes steeply down to the water's edge. The 1.5km stretch to where there is a shelter at the viewpoint is predominantly flat, although shade is limited and it is advisable to bring sun protection. Interesting features include granite

View of Anse Major and the coastline of the Morne Seychelles National Park.

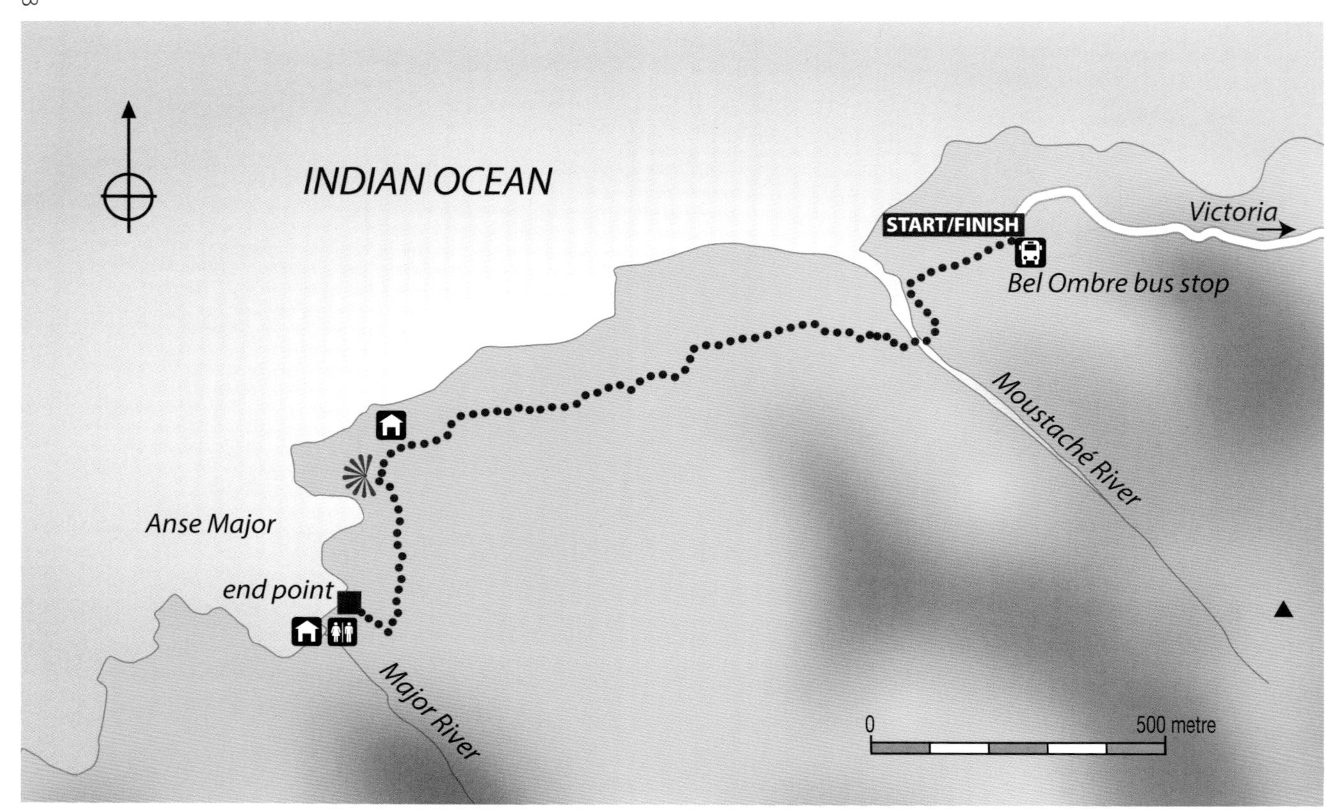
INDIAN OCEAN
START/FINISH
Victoria
Bel Ombre bus stop
Moustaché River
Anse Major
end point
Major River
0
500 metre

The trail winds along the coastline with views to the north towards Silhouette Island.

rock formations, which you will pass beneath, and small streams running down the glacis. However, be careful not to stray from the path as the rocks can be slippery and in some places the glacis run sharply downwards. Wild Pineapple and Vanilla can be found growing along the side of the path, and although the invasive Cocoplum is the dominant species of flora present, you will also encounter endemics, including Dillenia.

On arrival at the shelter, you will be rewarded with a view of Anse Major. From here it is a short walk down to the bay, which is made up of two beaches divided by some large rocks. As you approach the second, larger beach, you will encounter a freshwater pool on your left, which is excellent for a swim after you have been in the ocean. There are toilet facilities at the end of the beach, and for anyone not wanting to make the return journey on foot, it is sometimes possible to arrange a return trip to Bel Ombre harbour on a taxi-boat.

Waves break on Anse Major beach. Get there early to beat the crowds.

Casse Dent trail

SPECTACULAR TRAIL THROUGH THE FOREST

Level Advanced
Distance 8.2km
Time 4 hours
Getting there By car on the Sans Souci Road. By bus from Victoria (14) towards Port Launay.

The Casse Dent trail is one of the least visited of the trails on Mahé and you are more than likely to have it to yourself. However, the trail is relatively long and the challenging terrain makes this one for experienced hikers.

The trail begins on Sans Souci Road not far from the Mission Lodge. There is a sign by the side of the road marking the start of the trail, which ascends through the forest before sloping downwards through native palms. Keep an eye open for tree frogs on the palms, particularly near running water. Continuing along the trail, you will arrive at an area of Horne's Pandanus growing among the granite boulders. You will then cross several ravines and small streams, which often burst their banks during the rainy season. The footbridges, which traverse the ravines, are often slippery, so take care with your footing. Along the side of the path you should see several native and endemic plant species, including a variety of small orchids.

The trail slopes upwards once more until you leave the forest, arriving around the 4km

 The Seychelles Tree Frog is often found close to streams.

Mahé Island

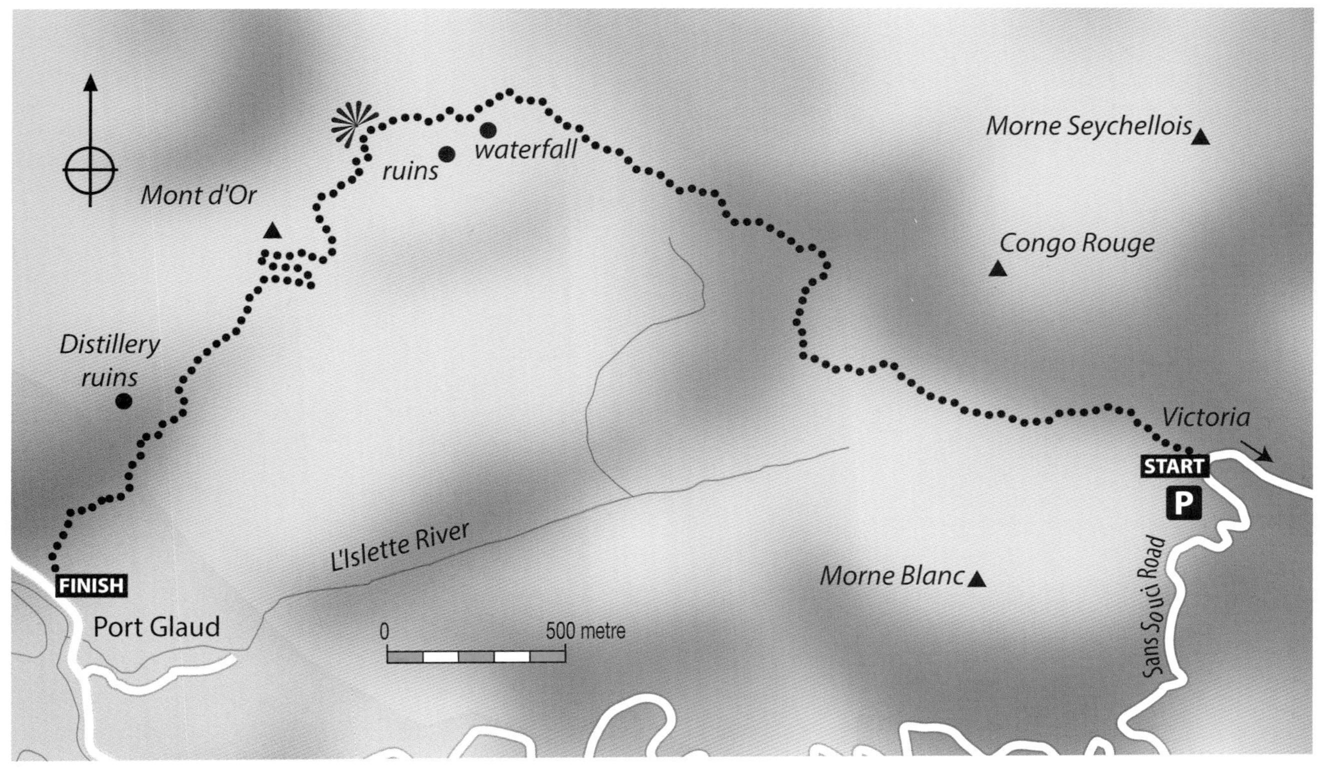
Mont d'Or
ruins
waterfall
Morne Seychellois
Congo Rouge
Distillery ruins
Victoria
START
P
FINISH
Port Glaud
L'Islette River
Morne Blanc
Sans Souci Road
0
500 metre

Bird's Nest Ferns grow from an endemic palm within the forest.

mark at a glacis with views of the west coast of Mahé and Morne Blanc on the left. From here you head downwards towards Port Glaud, passing the waterfall, where you can stop, cool down and have a swim. Feeling refreshed, it is time for the final descent. From here the route continues towards Port Glaud, where you will encounter the ruins of an old still, which was once part of a distillery. The next part of the trail can be challenging, as you need to climb over granite boulders, making sure to follow the markings painted on their surfaces.

You eventually reach a small path, which after passing through thick vegetation opens up to reveal an uninterrupted view of Port Glaud and Port Launay, as well as Thérèse Island. From here, you continue through old ruins and remnant gardens, keeping left towards Port Glaud. The trail leads to another glacis before opening on to a grassy path, which winds through a residential area. As you walk past several houses surrounded by fruit trees, you finally arrive at the main road opposite the football field. From here, it is possible to catch a bus back to Victoria and the east coast.

Copolia trail

MAGNIFICENT VIEWS OF THE EAST COAST OF MAHÉ AND THE STE ANNE MARINE NATIONAL PARK

Level Beginner
Distance 3.2km (return trip)
Time 1.5 hours
Getting there: By car on the Sans Souci Road. By bus from Victoria (14) towards Port Launay.

The Copolia trail is one of the most popular on Mahé and can sometimes become busy at the weekends.

From Victoria, take the Sans Souci Road. After a few kilometres you will arrive at the Copolia Lodge. Park at the side of the road and the trail begins next to the office facilities. There is a SCR100 entrance fee for non-residents.

The first part of the trail takes you through secondary forest, passing over small streams as you wind your way through the valley. Before long, the path begins a steep ascent towards the summit. Posts indicate the distance remaining at 200m intervals,

The Seychelles Parks and Gardens Authority building at the start of the trail.

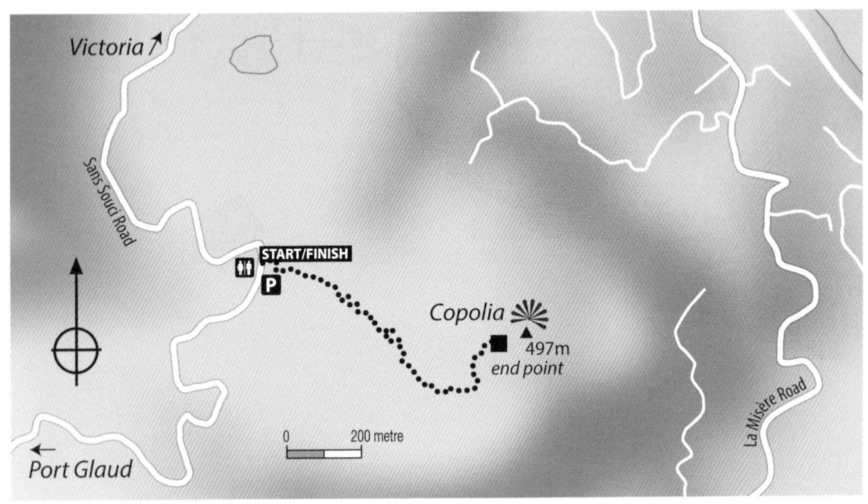

 The endemic Seychelles Pitcher Plants are widespread on the top of the glacis.

The glacis at the summit of the Copolia trail offers views of the east coast of Mahé, including Eden Island and the Ste Anne Marine National Park.

as you make your way through the forest. The introduced Cinnamon remains the dominant tree, while native ferns and endemic palms, including *Phoenicophorium borsigianum* and *Verschaffeltia splendida*, make up the undergrowth.

Continuing upwards, you need to navigate your way over boulders and cross over a couple of small bridges. Look out for Dillenia and other endemic plants as you get closer to the summit. At the end of the trail you arrive at some large granite boulders with a small ladder leading to the top of Copolia.

Once on the granite plateau, you are welcomed by magnificent views of the east coast of Mahé, as well as the surrounding peaks of Trois Frères, Morne Seychellois and Morne Blanc. In the distance, beyond the Ste Anne Marine National Park, you can see Praslin and La Digue on a clear day.

Take time to explore the granite plateau, where you can find plenty of endemic Seychelles Pitcher Plants and Mountain Pandanus. A covered seating area provides an opportunity to rest and take in the spectacular views.

The route down is the same, although much quicker. Be careful, particularly if it has been raining, as the terrain can become hazardous.

Dan Gallas trail

PANORAMIC VIEWS

Level Intermediate
Distance 5.8km (return trip)
Time 2 hours 30 minutes
Getting there By bus (32) from Victoria (le Niol bus stop). By car if travelling from Victoria, head towards Beau Vallon, before taking the road on the left towards Le Niol.

The Dan Gallas trail is named after the Ethiopian people (the Gallas) who were liberated by the British from Arab dhows in the nineteenth century and settled in the area.

If coming by car, there is parking for a couple of vehicles a little further down the road. The start of the trail is opposite the bus stop behind the Seychelles National Parks Authority office. The path begins with a number of concrete steps, before switching to a muddy trail lined with endemic palms. This is a good location to search for the Tiger Chameleon, which is particularly active in the early evening when it climbs down from the higher tree branches.

Follow the trail upwards until you reach a dirt road. Take a left and follow the signs towards Dan Gallas, until you reach some telephone antennae. Here you will have an

The Seychelles Skink is one of the most common lizards found within the granitic islands.

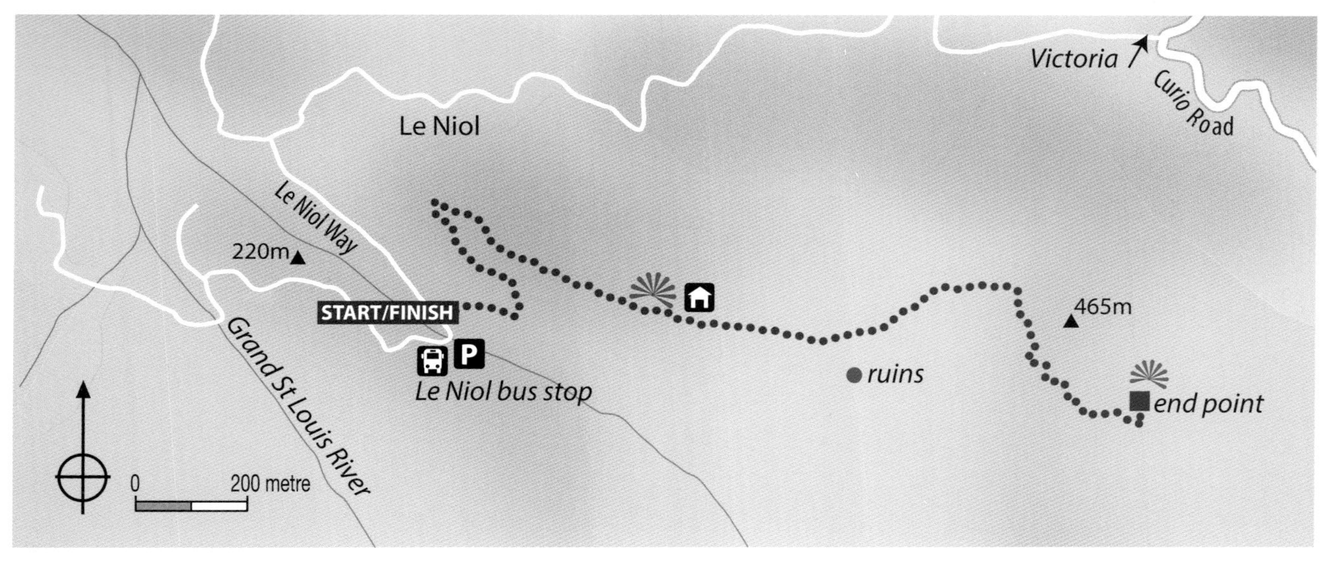
Le Niol
Victoria
Curio Road
Le Niol Way
220m
START/FINISH
Grand St Louis River
Le Niol bus stop
ruins
465m
end point
0
200 metre

incredible view of Beau Vallon bay and the north-west coast of Mahé. Although the dirt road continues to the left, take the path to the right, which climbs upwards to Dan Gallas. As you climb higher, you have further opportunities to see Beau Vallon bay below and Silhouette Island. After 30 minutes you reach a small shelter with a picnic table, where you can rest from the ascent.

Once you are ready to resume the hike, continue to follow the path, as a forest dominated by introduced Cinnamon trees replaces the scrub-like vegetation. Eventually you arrive at a large granite boulder and metal ladder. Climb the ladder to the top of the plateau, making use of the railings along the way. From the top of the rocky outcrop there are views of the east coast, including the port of Victoria and the St Anne Marine National Park. Retrace your steps to return to the start.

 View of Beau Vallon and the north coast of Mahé.

La Réserve trail

PALM FORESTS, IMPRESSIVE GRANITE BOULDERS AND STUNNING VIEWS

Level Beginner
Distance 1.8km (return trip)
Time 1 hour
Getting there By car take the Montagne Posée road to Bon Espoir. By bus from Victoria station.

The La Réserve trail is the ideal hike for those who only have a couple of hours to spare and is perfect for people of all abilities.

If coming by car, there is parking next to the Cable and Wireless station. Located within the Montagne Posée range in the south of the island, the start of the trail begins near the Cable and Wireless station. The forest around the beginning of the trail is a mixture of endemic palms and introduced Cinnamon trees. Pineapple plants are found along the sides of the path, while wild Vanilla grows around palms and other trees.

The path continues through the forest for approximately 700m, before ending at a large open glacis. From here the path disappears and you have to follow the markings

The first part of the trail passes through forest.

Montagne Posée Road
243m
Anse Boileau
P
START/FINISH
Bon Espoir
Anse aux Pins
265m
end point
0
200 metre
Monte Brûlée

From the top of the glacis you can see Montagne Posée prison in the distance.

painted on to the granite boulders to reach your destination. As you cross the glacis, you can see a collection of buildings on a plateau in the distance. This is the main prison facility for Seychelles, with capacity for more than 750 prisoners. The open expanse of the glacis provides the opportunity to watch the Seychelles Fruit Bat flying above the forest canopy.

Continue along the top of the glacis, being very careful not to fall in the ravines between the granite boulders. Eventually you reach a rocky promontory, on which is located an observation deck. The platform offers views overlooking Anse Boileau and the east coast of Mahé. On a clear day you can also make out Praslin and La Digue on the horizon. This is the ideal place to rest, take in the scenery and enjoy the cool breeze.

The return hike back to Bon Espoir is a short and easy one, crossing back across the glacis top before rejoining the forest trail.

Seychelles Fruit Bats are common on the larger granitic islands.

Mare aux Cochons trail

THROUGH FOREST AND WETLANDS WITH PLENTY OF OPPORTUNITIES FOR VIEWING WILDLIFE

Level Intermediate to Advanced
Distance 9.5km (return trip)
Time: 6 hours
Getting there If beginning the trail at Le Niol: by car, take the Victoria to Beau Vallon road, turn left towards Le Niol and park at the last bus stop (the trail starts on your left); by bus from Victoria, disembark at the last bus stop. If beginning the trail from Danzil: by car, drive through Bel Ombre continuing until you see a sign on the left for Mare aux Cochons. Follow the road upwards for 2km and park on the right-hand side not far from the poultry farm; by bus, disembark at the Bel Ombre bus terminus opposite the La Scala restaurant and walk the final few kilometres to the start of the trail.

Mare aux Cochons is a series of interlinked trails located in the Morne Seychellois National Park. The moderately difficult trails can be accessed from either Danzil in Bel Ombre, or Le Niol on the road between Beau Vallon and Victoria. Mare aux Cochons is actually the name of the upland marsh found along the trail, and it is officially the world's second smallest Ramsar Site.

Beginning at Danzil, there is a signpost that reads 'Dans Bernard'. From here it is a steep climb through dense forest. The narrow, winding route eventually meets a wider path, which forks towards Mare aux Cochons to the right and Le Niol to the left. The remainder of the hike has less of an incline, and passes through upland forest before arriving at the wetland. There is a small wooden shelter with seating next to the marsh, the perfect place to have a picnic lunch and watch dragonflies fly by. From here the trail continues through a pandanus forest before sloping downwards towards Port Glaud. Alternatively, you can turn around and head back the way you came.

Screwpines surround the wetland at the top of the trail.

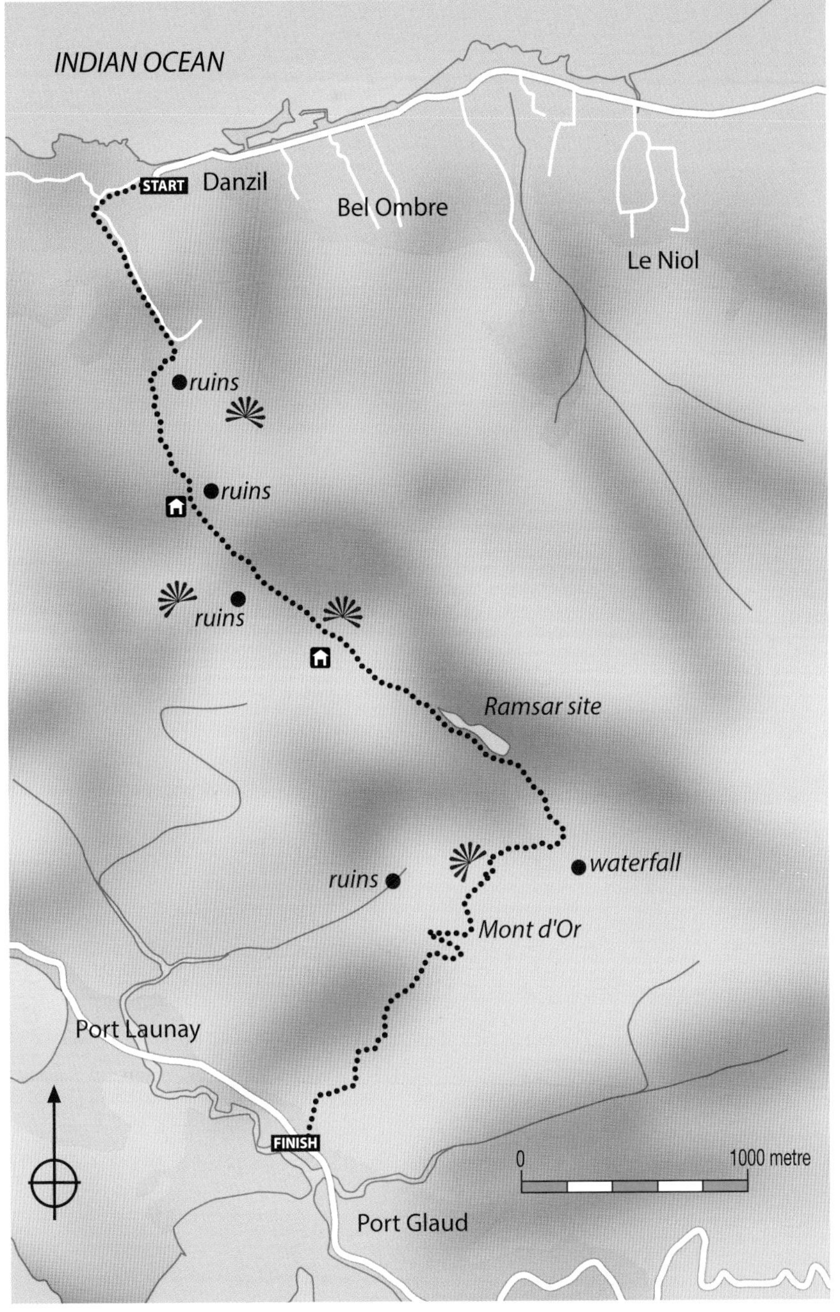
INDIAN OCEAN
START
Danzil
Bel Ombre
Le Niol
ruins
ruins
ruins
Ramsar site
waterfall
ruins
Mont d'Or
Port Launay
FINISH
0
1000 metre
Port Glaud

One of a number of small waterfalls to be found along the trail.

Depending on your pace, the trail takes between four and six hours. Highlights include several small historical ruins, mountain streams and native wildlife. Take a towel if you fancy a dip in one of the refreshing mountain streams, and remember to bring plenty of drinking water. Keep your eyes open for tree frogs and snakes near the marsh, and for native orchids alongside the path. You will also see plenty of Golden Panchax, an endemic freshwater fish, in the clear running streams.

The Seychelles Wolf Snake can be found in trees lining the path.

Morne Blanc trail

A STEEP CLIMB UP THE WHITE MOUNTAIN FOR INCREDIBLE VIEWS

Level Intermediate
Distance 6.4km (return trip)
Time 1 hour 20 minutes
Getting there By bus (no. 14) from Victoria bus terminal stopping next to the sign for the start of the trail located at the side of the road. By car follow the Sans Souci road for approximately 10km.

Situated along Sans Souci Road above the Tea Factory, the trail begins by the side of the road and makes its way up steeply through thick forest.

If coming by car, there is enough parking space for a couple of vehicles opposite the Tea Factory, located a further 200m along the road from the sign marking the trail. The forest along the trail rises from 200m to approximately 400m, and is dominated by introduced Cinnamon trees. Nevertheless, the undergrowth contains plenty of endemics, including the different palm species with their spiny trunks. Wildlife found along the trail includes stick insects and the Black Dancing Snail. Usually found on the endemic palms, these small black snails shake their shells from side to side if you gently touch them.

The trail continues upwards and passes through some large granite boulders. At this elevation it is often misty (particularly later in the day), and this is reflected in

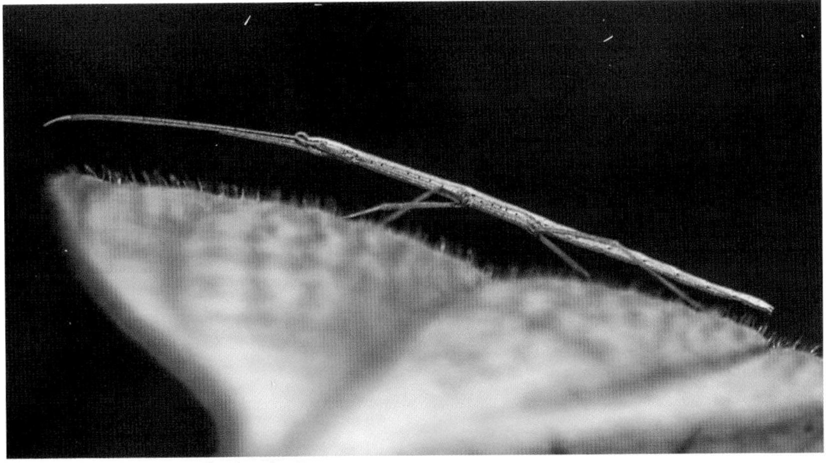

A stick insect sits upon a leaf in the forest.

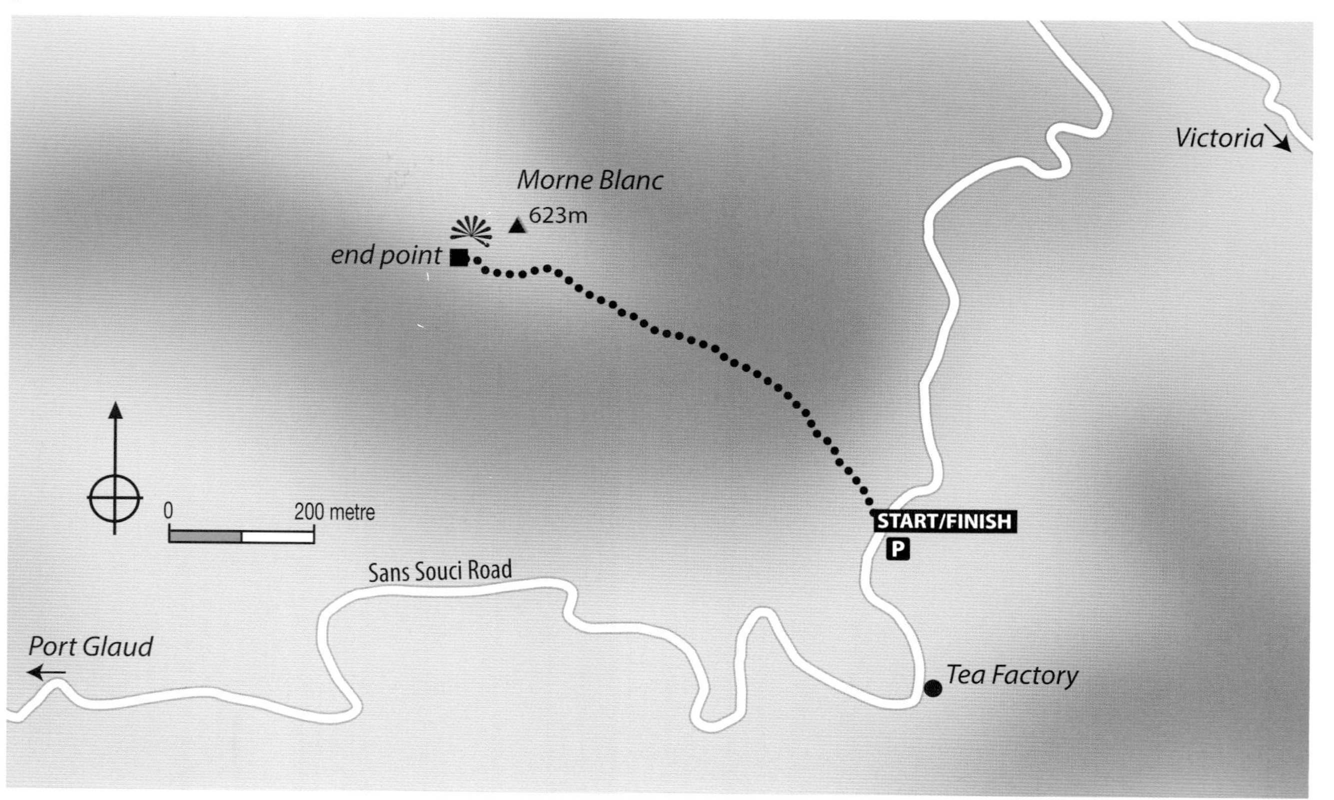
Morne Blanc
623m
end point
Victoria
0
200 metre
START/FINISH
P
Sans Souci Road
Port Glaud
Tea Factory

a change in the vegetation. The atmosphere is much more humid and the tree trunks are covered in thick layers of moss and lichens, giving the forest a mystical feel. In between the boulders there are deep crevices, and short boardwalks have been built to navigate them. Make sure you stay on the trail to avoid the possibility of falling into one of these openings.

The trees at higher altitudes towards the end of the trail are covered in thick layers of moss.

When you reach the summit, you pass along a series of small bridges leading to a wooden observation platform. From here you are greeted by an incredible view of the west coast of Mahé, including the islands of Île aux Vaches, Thérèse and Conception. To the south you can see Anse Boileau and Baie Lazare, while to the north are Port Launay and Baie Ternay. This is the perfect spot to take a break and have a bite to eat before making the journey back down.

The descent back down the trail tends to be much quicker, but take care not to fall, as it can be slippery underfoot, particularly if it has been raining.

The view of the north-west coast, including Therese and Conception Islands.

Trois Frères trail

ENDEMIC PITCHER PLANTS AND SPECTACULAR VIEWS OVERLOOKING VICTORIA AND THE EAST COAST

Level Beginner
Distance 2.8km (return trip)
Time 1 hour 10 minutes
Getting there By bus from Victoria, Sans Souci Forestry Station stop, then follow the sign on the opposite side of the road leading to the start of the trail. By car from Victoria.

The name Trois Frères (three brothers) refers to the three closely situated peaks that rise above Victoria. This is a short yet steep hike that offers views of the east coast of Mahé.

Travelling along the San Souci Road from Victoria, turn left after 5km at the sign passing through a housing estate until you arrive at a cul-de-sac where you can park the car and begin the trail. There is space here to park a vehicle or two,

Initially you pass through a forested area containing many introduced species, including Cinnamon and Santol, until you reach the first viewpoint overlooking Victoria and the east coast. As you continue further along the trail, you start to see a few endemic plant species, including endemic palms and the occasional pandanus. Look out for endemic birds including the Seychelles Bulbul and Seychelles Blue Pigeon.

Before long the soil is replaced by large paving slabs, and eventually you exit the forest. Bushes of the introduced Cocoplum border the trail, and you encounter a steep glacis. Follow the steps upwards, making

A huge granite boulder stands above the forest.

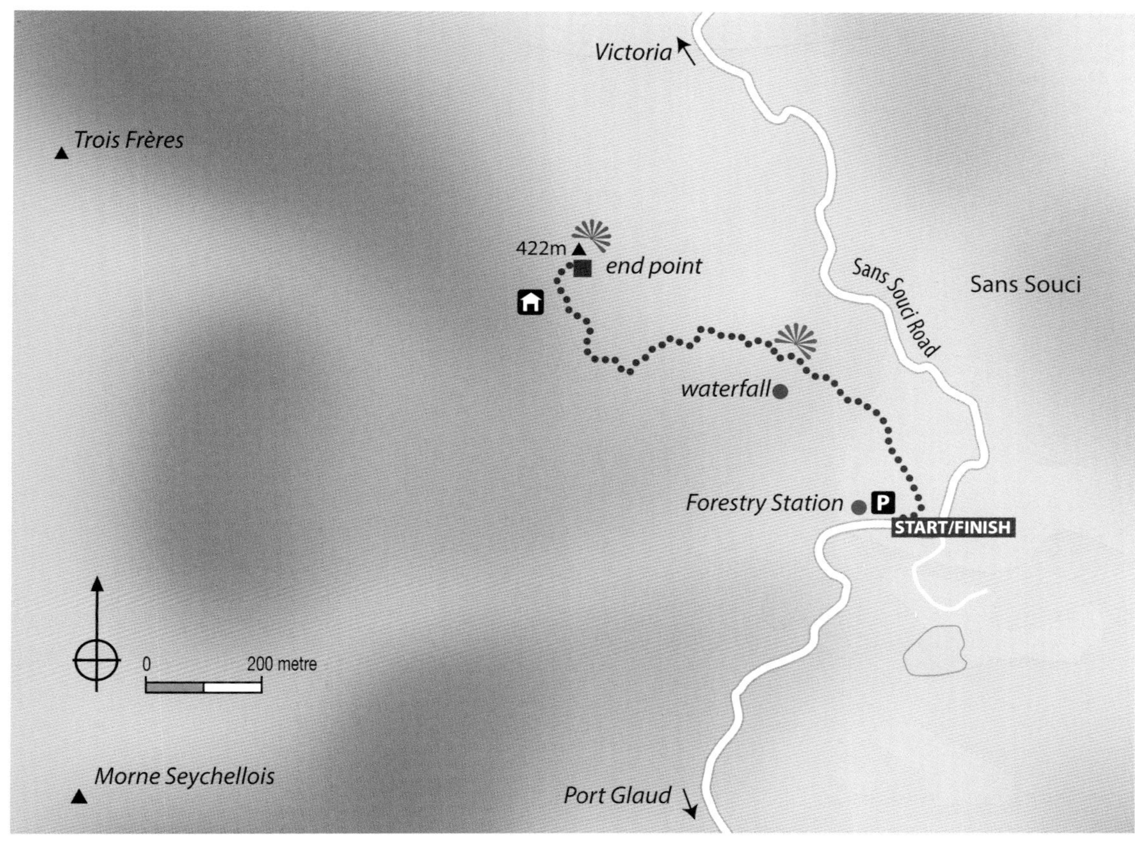
Victoria
Trois Frères
422m
end point
Sans Souci Road
Sans Souci
waterfall
Forestry Station
P
START/FINISH
0
200 metre
Morne Seychellois
Port Glaud

Seychelles Pitcher Plants grow on the glacis at the top of the trail.

use of the hand rail. Once on top of the glacis pay attention to the signs that direct you towards the path on your right to locate the Seychelles Pitcher Plants. Do not take the path to the left, as although it leads to the Trois Frères cross, it is not well maintained and unsuitable for hiking. Next to the pitcher plants there is a rocky outcrop and a wooden shelter where you can enjoy stunning views of Victoria and the St Anne Marine National Park.

The return journey is back down the way you came up and can be steep in places, so take care with your footing.

 Insects, such as ants, are attracted to the pitcher plants.

PRASLIN ISLAND

Praslin is the second largest and next most densely populated of the islands after Mahé. The island is named after Gabriel de Choiseul, Duc de Praslin, a French minister of marine affairs from the eighteenth century. The island is much quieter than Mahé and has plenty of attractions for the hiker and wildlife enthusiast.

Over the years forest fires and deforestation have greatly reduced the amount of original forest area on the island. However, Praslin's palm forests include the UNESCO World Heritage Site of the Vallée de Mai, stronghold of the endemic Coco-de-mer palm and one of the best places to see the Seychelles Black Parrot.

There are numerous places for hiking through the forests of Praslin, including the Salazie, Pasquière and Glacis Noire trails, and the Fond Ferdinand Nature Reserve. The streams of Praslin are home to eels and freshwater crabs, and you will occasionally find tree frogs on the leaves of native palms. The Giant Bronze Gecko is only found in the Vallée de Mai, which is also home to the Tiger Chameleon.

Away from the forested peaks, Praslin is blessed with some of the most beautiful beaches to be found in Seychelles. Anse Lazio is frequently ranked in lists of the world's best beaches, while in truth any of the dozens of palm-fringed stretches of white sand to be found on the island could easily qualify. On the more remote beaches you are likely to encounter the tracks of sea turtles during the nesting season.

Granite boulders along the coast of Praslin Island.

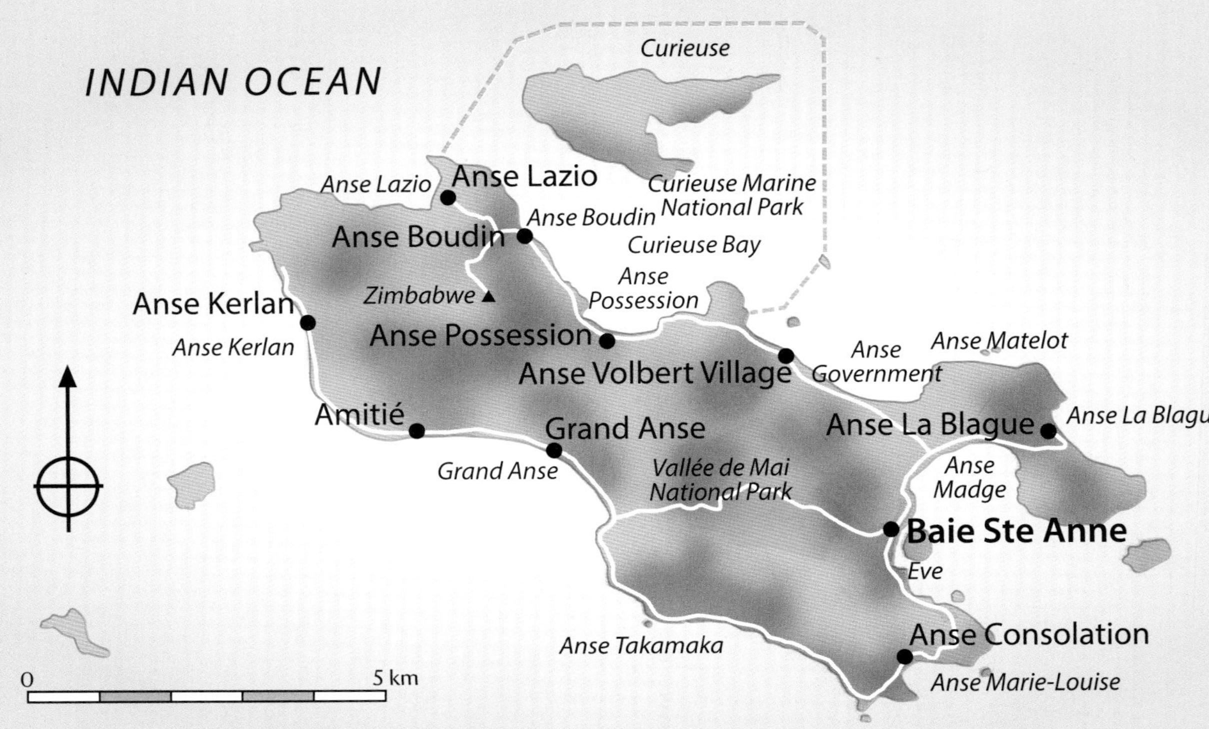
INDIAN OCEAN
Curieuse
Anse Lazio
Anse Lazio
Curieuse Marine National Park
Anse Boudin
Anse Boudin
Curieuse Bay
Anse Possession
Zimbabwe
Anse Kerlan
Anse Kerlan
Anse Possession
Anse Volbert Village
Anse Government
Anse Matelot
Amitié
Grand Anse
Grand Anse
Vallée de Mai National Park
Anse La Blague
Anse La Blague
Anse Madge
Baie Ste Anne
Eve
Anse Takamaka
Anse Consolation
Anse Marie-Louise
0
5 km

Anse Georgette & Anse Lazio trail

STEEP CLIMBS AND BEAUTIFUL BEACHES

Level Intermediate
Distance 7km (return trip)
Time 3 hours
Getting there By car, park near the Constance Lemuria Hotel.

This hike will take you through coastal forest to visit two of Seychelles most beautiful beaches (in Seychelles, 'anse' *refers to a beach).*

From the hotel, walk along the paved road towards Newcome House. As you continue upwards, the paved road becomes a track and you reach a ridge with views of the Indian Ocean, with Aride Island in the distance. The track comes to an end and you need to start the descent towards Anse Lazio below. Passing through palm forest with occasional Breadfruit trees and huge granite boulders, keep heading downwards until the incline becomes less steep and you arrive at the pristine stretch of beach surrounded by turquoise water. The beach stretches 600m across the bay with numerous huge, red granite boulders lying in the shallow water close to shore. There are a few shops and restaurants at either end of the beach, so it is possible to grab something to eat after you have been for a swim in the warm Indian Ocean.

When you are ready to leave, you need to head back the way you came. Although the climb can be challenging, it does not take long and you soon find yourself back

The picture-perfect Anse Lazio.

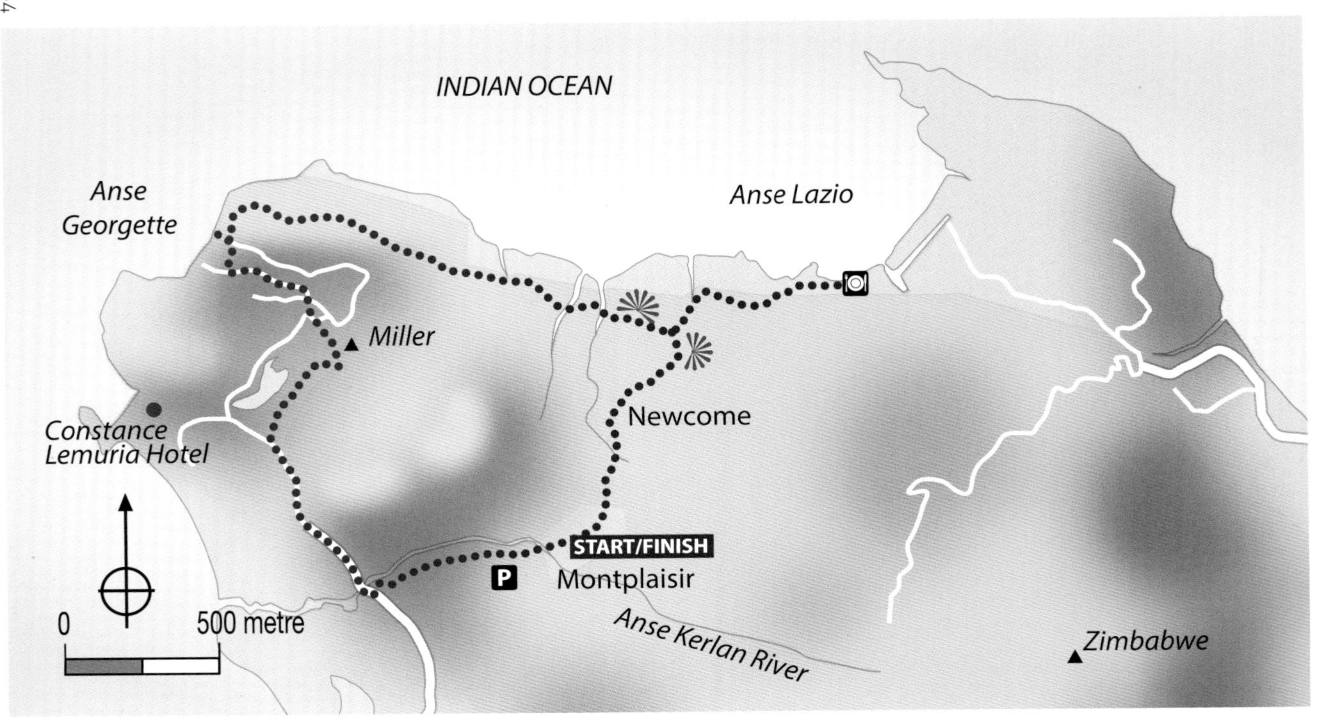
INDIAN OCEAN
Anse
Georgette
Anse Lazio
Miller
Newcome
Constance
Lemuria Hotel
START/FINISH
P
Montplaisir
0
500 metre
Anse Kerlan River
Zimbabwe

on the paved road. From here, follow the trail through a Coco-de-mer grove, climbing over a peak before descending to the coast and Anse Georgette. The trail passes through dense forest and fluctuates between upwards climbs and subsequent descents. There is no signage on this part of the trail, so it is important to pay attention to where you are heading. When you exit the forest, continue along the path until you reach a fork, making sure you keep to the right, then take a left at the following junction towards Anse Georgette. You begin a steep descent with ocean views, until you reach the little beach of Anse Georgette below. Although much smaller than Anse Lazio, Anse Georgette is equally stunning and tends to be much quieter than its more famous neighbour. It lacks nearby facilities, except for those belonging to the Constance Lemuria Hotel. Sea turtles nest on Anse Georgette during the breeding season.

The endemic Seychelles Bulbul can be quite inquisitive.

Unless you are a guest at the Constance Lemuria Hotel and that is your final destination, you make the return journey back up the headland and follow the trail back to your original starting point.

Coconut palms provide shade on the beach.

Fond Ferdinand trail

HIKING THROUGH A NATURE RESERVE RICH IN ENDEMIC PLANT AND ANIMAL SPECIES

Level Beginner
Distance 4–6km
Time 1–3 hours
Getting there By car from Baie Sainte Anne, take the Anse Marie Louise road turning right at the sign for Fond Ferdinand. By bus, disembark at the sign for Fond Ferdinand.

The Fond Ferdinand ravine is located in the south of Praslin, with the entrance just off the coastal road opposite Anse Marie Louise beach.

If coming by bus, you need to walk the short distance to the entrance and ticket office on the opposite side of the road to the beach. Those driving can find ample parking at the entrance.

Under the management of the Seychelles Islands Foundation since 2020, Fond Ferdinand covers 1.5km^2 of palm forest and is open seven days a week from 9 a.m. to

Coco-de-Mer nuts piled up near the entrance to Fond Ferdinand.

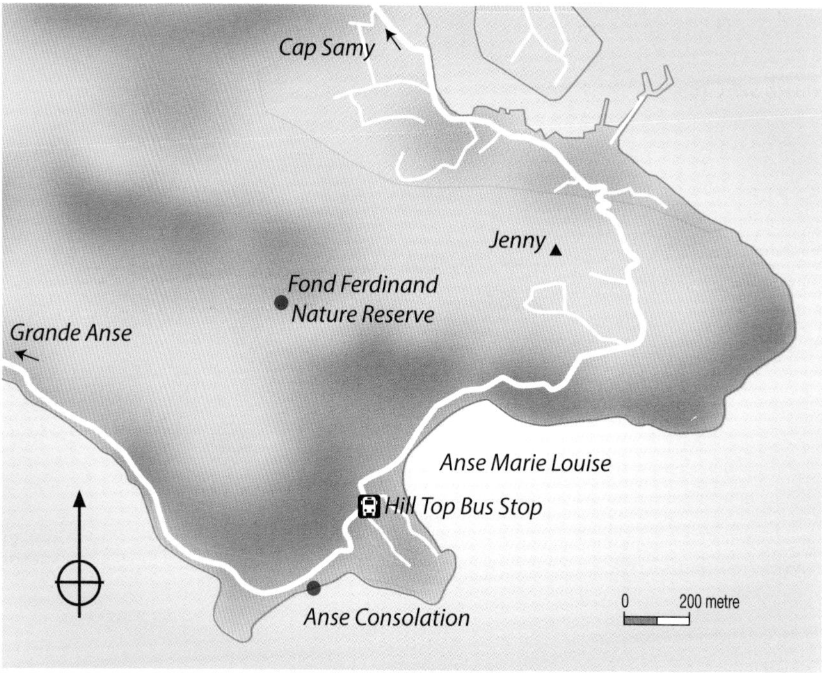

Cap Samy
Jenny
Fond Ferdinand Nature Reserve
Grande Anse
Anse Marie Louise
Hill Top Bus Stop
Anse Consolation
0 200 metre

Coco-de-Mer palms within the forest.

At the top of the trail the forest opens out, leading to views of the Praslin coast.

1 p.m. The forest was restored after a fire destroyed the former palm plantation in 1990. Today it is home to a majestic forest of Coco-de-mer palms, which is easily accessed along well-maintained paths.

On arrival you are required to buy a ticket to enter the forest, after which you are assigned a professional guide. Look out for freshwater shrimps and eels in the clear streams that pass by the entrance. The hike departs in one of two directions and winds its way through the forest up the hillside. The Coco-de-mer palms are not as tall here as they are in the Vallée de Mai, making it easier to get a good look at some of their enormous nuts. As you climb higher, you leave the forest and join a more open area where the red soil becomes exposed. At the summit you can stop to catch your breath and enjoy the views of Félicité and La Digue islands in the distance.

While it is possible to turn around at this point and head back the way you climbed, the path also carries on down the other side of the mountain and back through the valley. You once again descend into palm forest, where your knowledgeable guide will point out plants of interest, providing you with information about their biology. Depending on your pace and how often you stop, a hike within Fond Ferdinand can take anywhere between one and three hours.

Vallée de Mai trail

HIKE AMONG SOME OF THE RAREST SPECIES IN THE WORLD AMIDST INCREDIBLE SCENERY

Level Beginner
Distance 2–4km
Time 1–2 hours
Getting there By car from Baie Sainte Anne, follow the main road that traverses the island until you reach the Vallée de Mai. This is also the stopping-off point for buses travelling in both directions.

The Vallée de Mai is a 0.20km² palm forest located in the centre of Praslin Island, along the main road that connects the villages of Baie Sainte Anne and Grande Anse. A nature reserve since the 1960s, in 1983 the Vallée de Mai was designated a UNESCO World Heritage Site due to it being the best preserved forest for the endangered Coco-de-mer palm, an endemic palm that is only found growing naturally on Praslin and Curieuse Islands. Today the site is managed by the Seychelles Islands Foundation.

The entrance is located on the main road, where there is also a car park and bus stop. You arrive at the visitor centre, which has a shop, cafeteria and some toilets. This is where you can purchase your ticket for entry into the reserve. On entering the forest you see a small display table, which contains an example of one of the mighty Coco-de-mer nuts, as well as a male inflorescence.

An aerial view of the Vallée de Mai palm forest.

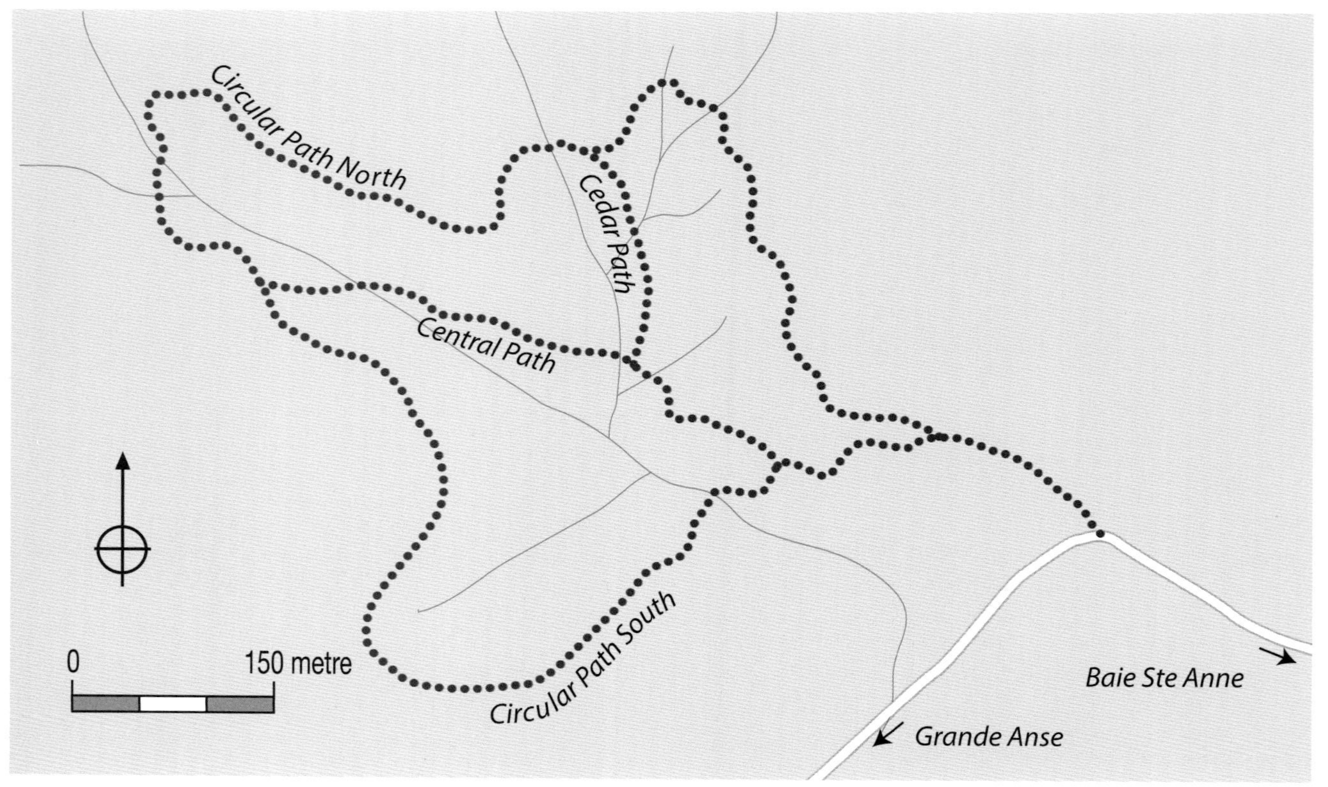
Circular Path North
Cedar Path
Central Path
Circular Path South
0
150 metre
Baie Ste Anne
Grande Anse

Keep on the lookout for the Seychelles Tiger Chameleon, which is found within the forest.

There are three different routes in the forest, ranging from 1km to 2km in length – the Circular Path (North and South), the Central Path and the Cedar Path. All three routes lead back to the entrance of the park. Along the well-maintained paths there are plenty of places to stop and sit, so it is possible to spend as much time as you like taking in the incredible scenery. For those wanting to learn more about the biodiversity of the forest, private guides can be hired, or it is possible to join a group tour.

The Coco-de-mer palms grow taller in the Vallée de Mai than in neighbouring forests, and the reserve is home to all three species of bronze gecko, including the Giant Bronze Gecko. The forest is also home to the Tiger Chameleon, which can sometimes be seen dangling from the fronds of endemic palms.

Listen out for the Seychelles Black Parrot, often heard before it is seen. In fact, the best chance of gaining an unobstructed view of these rare birds is often in the car park outside the visitor centre. The paths and boardwalks within the Vallée de Mai pass over several shallow streams, which contain the endemic Praslin Freshwater Crab, and a variety of insects can be found among the leaf litter.

The Seychelles Islands Foundation is conducting intensive field studies of many species found in the forest. This should help to better understand their biology and behaviour, with a view to ensuring their long-term conservation.

The paths within the forest are well maintained.

SILHOUETTE ISLAND

Silhouette Island is the third largest of the granitic islands. It covers an area of 20km^2 and is home to Seychelles' second highest peak, Mt Dauban, at a height of 740m. In 1609, the crew from an English East India Company ship were the first recorded visitors to the island.

Together with neighbouring North Island, Silhouette is made up of syenite (a course-grained intrusive igneous rock with a general composition similar to granite, but deficient in quartz), and is much younger than the other islands within the granitic group. The island remains densely forested and retains pockets of primary forest. In 2010, 93 per cent of the island was declared a national park, and today it is under the active management of the Island Conservation Society (ICS).

Access to the island is by boat from Bel Ombre on Mahé. It is possible to visit for the day, but for those intending to hike across the island, staying at one of the two hotel establishments is recommended.

Silhouette is rich in biodiversity, including endemic plants, birds and reptiles. The island is home to a population of Sheath-tailed Bats, which are listed on the IUCN Red List as Critically Endangered, with fewer than 100 individuals remaining. Amphibian species include the Seychelles Tree Frog, Thomasset's Frog and the Seychelles Palm Frog, which is endemic to Silhouette.

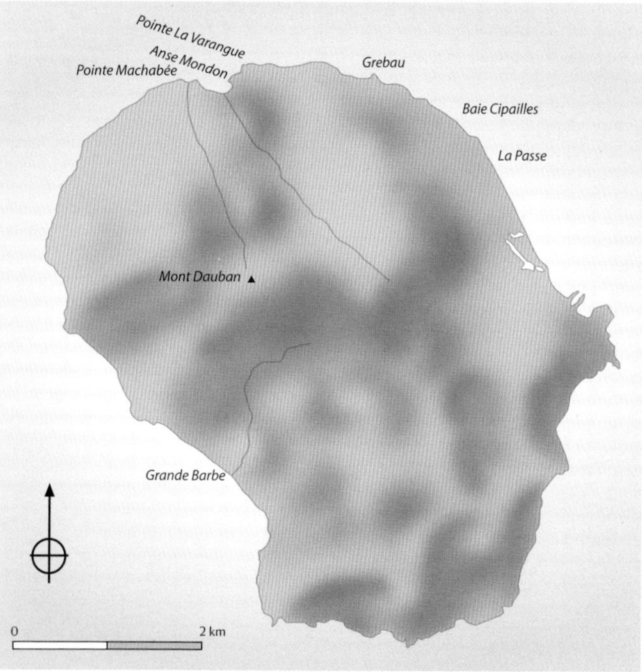

While most of the island is heavily forested, it also boasts some beautiful deserted beaches. Grande Barbe is an important nesting beach for Hawksbill Turtles, and the adjacent wetlands and mangrove forest provide nursery grounds for a variety of marine life.

Anse Mondon trail

THROUGH LUSH FOREST AND UNSPOILED NATURAL VEGETATION

Level Intermediate
Distance 6.4km (return trip)
Time 3 hours
Getting there: By ferry from Bel Ombre, Mahé.

The Anse Mondon trail is located on the north-east coast of Silhouette Island.

To access the trail you need to walk through the village at La Passe and the grounds of the Hilton Hotel, until you reach the beach at Baie Cipailles. A further 500m along the beach you come to a sign that indicates the start of the trail.

Leaving the beach behind you, the trail slopes upwards through a dense forest of Coconut trees. After 500m the Coconut palms begin to thin out and Cinnamon trees become more common. From this point onwards you are likely to encounter the Seychelles Giant Millipede at the bases of trees and among the leaf litter. Continue for a further 30 minutes until you reach another sign confirming that you are still heading in the right direction.

The sign marks the start of a trail through the forest towards Anse Mondon.

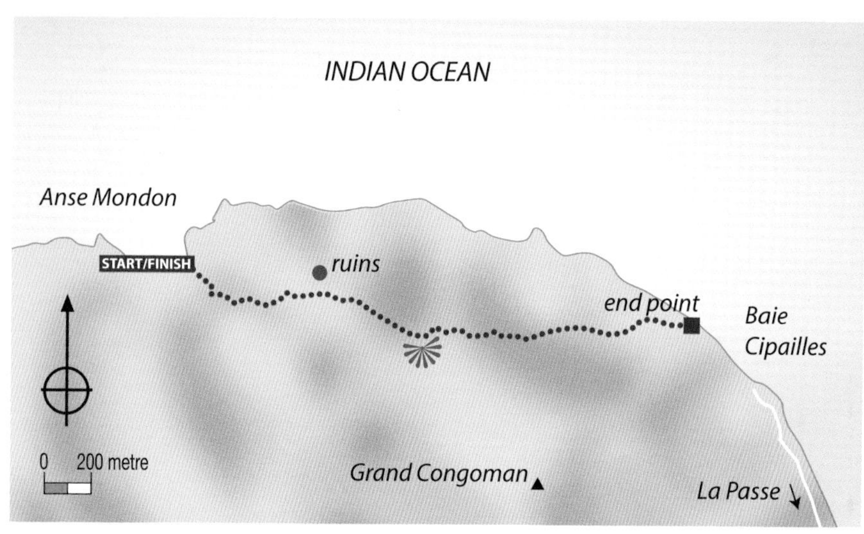

 A shallow stream passes through the forest next to the trail.

Exposed granite boulders at low tide.

On reaching the halfway point you get your first glimpse of the Indian Ocean to your right. Continue walking through the plateau until you begin a descent towards the coast. This section of the hike takes a little under an hour and you eventually arrive at a wooden bridge crossing a river. Down on the plateau you pass ruins of buildings that were once homes to people who farmed the area, and eventually travel through Coconut palms as you arrive at the secluded beach. At certain times of the year the sea can be rough, so be careful if you plan to swim. Anse Mondon is, however, the perfect spot to rest and have some lunch before you begin the return journey, which takes you along the same route.

Grande Barbe trail

A CHALLENGING TREK FROM THE EAST COAST TO THE WEST

Level Advanced
Distance 13km (return trip)
Time 6 hours
Getting there By ferry from Bel Ombre, Mahé.

The hike across Silhouette Island to Grande Barbe beach is without doubt one of the most challenging to be found in Seychelles. A return trip takes most of the day and the difficult terrain, combined with the heat, make this particular trail suitable only for experienced hikers. For those wanting a professional guide, they are available for hire on the island, but hikes will only proceed if the weather permits.

Beginning on the concrete road where the ferry drops off visitors, you make your way through the village at La Passe to the start of the trail, passing a small reservoir before turning left, then left again at a fork in the path. Continuing upwards through large granite boulders, the trail passes through forest until you reach the highest point of the hike at 400m above sea level.

The extensive wetland at Grande Barbe is lined by mangrove trees.

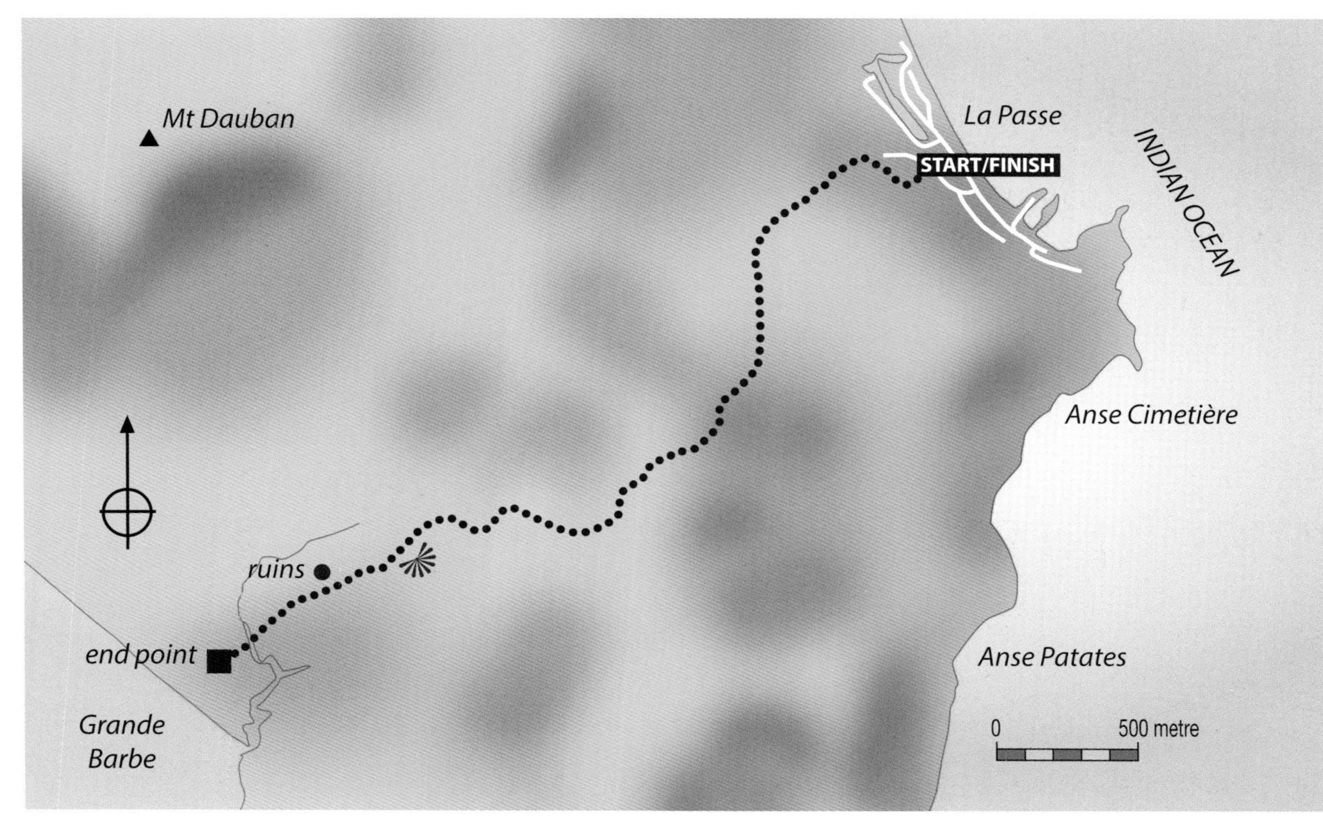
Mt Dauban
La Passe
START/FINISH
INDIAN OCEAN
Anse Cimetière
ruins
end point
Anse Patates
Grande
Barbe
0
500 metre

One of the 'A'-Frame buildings belonging to the Island Development Company.

Over the next 5km, the trail winds downwards as you pass through densely forested valleys full of endemic palms and introduced Cinnamon trees. Eventually you break out of the forest to find yourself in the open on granite boulders. From here you have your first glimpse of the ocean and a steep path, lined on each side by ferns, which works its way down the mountainside. Take care with your footing, as the soil can be loose, particularly after rain. After another 1km the vegetation turns to Coconut trees, providing some respite from the sun. The trees give way to a clearing as you arrive at what remains of the historic Grande Barbe village. The vegetation has reclaimed many of the old buildings, but the 'A' frames belonging to the Island Development Company are still in use.

Exiting the village, you arrive at the incredible Grande Barbe beach. As you face the sea, to your left are some of the best remaining mangroves to be found within the granitic islands, while to your right an immaculate stretch of white sand is overlooked by the imposing Mt Dauban. Take some time to swim in the ocean, eat your lunch, and gather your energy before making the long journey back to the other side of the island.

The stunning Grande Barbe beach with Mt Dauban in the background.

LA DIGUE ISLAND

Situated 4km east of Praslin, La Digue is the fourth largest and third most populated of the Seychelles islands. Like Mahé and Praslin, the island has many hotels and guest houses, with something to suit most people's tastes. La Digue is much more laid back than the other three islands, with ownership of motor vehicles restricted to business owners, and bicycles the preferred mode of transport.

The island is about 6km long and around 3km wide, with its highest point, Nid d'Aigle (Eagle's Nest), at 333m. The interior of the island is forested, and while the coastal plateaux have seen much development in recent years, the tiny Veuve Special Reserve remains a stronghold of the Seychelles Black Paradise Flycatcher, which can be easily seen in the forest.

La Digue is well known for its magnificent beaches, perhaps the most famous of which is Anse Source d'Argent, supposedly one of the most photographed beaches in the world. The beach is accessed through Union Estate (where an entrance fee must be paid), and by cycling through Coconut and Vanilla plantations. The beach itself comprises a series of smaller beaches bisected by huge pink granite boulders. Wade out into the shallow water and look back at the perfect white sand to really appreciate the beauty of the coastline.

Beyond Anse Source d'Argent is a series of more remote beaches, not as easily accessible, but equally beautiful. Few people venture this far and you are likely to have the beach to yourself.

While there are enjoyable hikes to be done on La Digue, cycling is definitely the preferred method of getting around, and it is possible to cycle along the coastal road from Union Estate in the west, to Anse Fourmis in the east, taking in the entire north coast of the island.

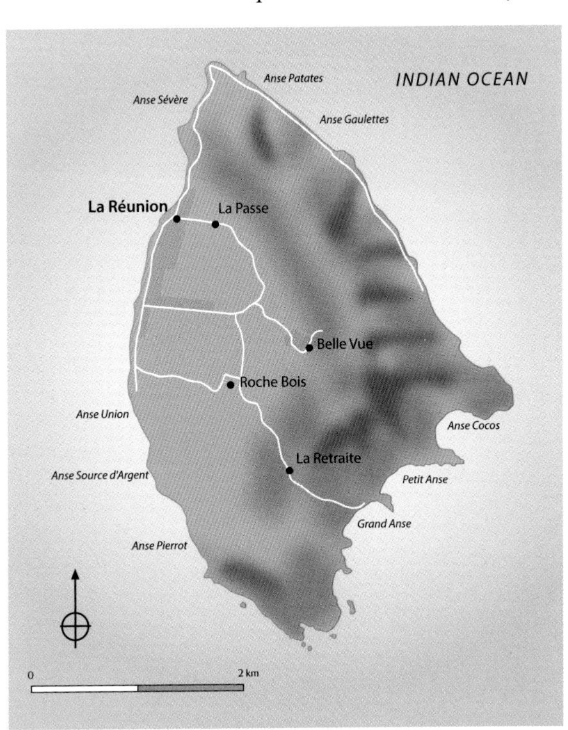

Nid D'Aigle trail

STUNNING VIEWS OVERLOOKING NEARBY ISLANDS

Level Beginner
Distance 2.6km (return trip)
Time 1 hour 20 minutes
Getting there By taxi from La Passe.

It is possible to start this hike from the La Passe, but doing so will add a significant distance to your journey, making it much more challenging. The easier alternative is to take a taxi to the start of the trail at the Belle Vue restaurant.

Outside the restaurant is a wooden sign that reads 'Mountain' and points you in the right direction. Follow the trail, making sure you continue straight ahead (do not take the fork to the right), passing through a forest made up of introduced Cinnamon trees. Be on the lookout for the Seychelles Skink scurrying along the forest floor, and listen

 The Seychelles Bulbul is a common sight along the trail.

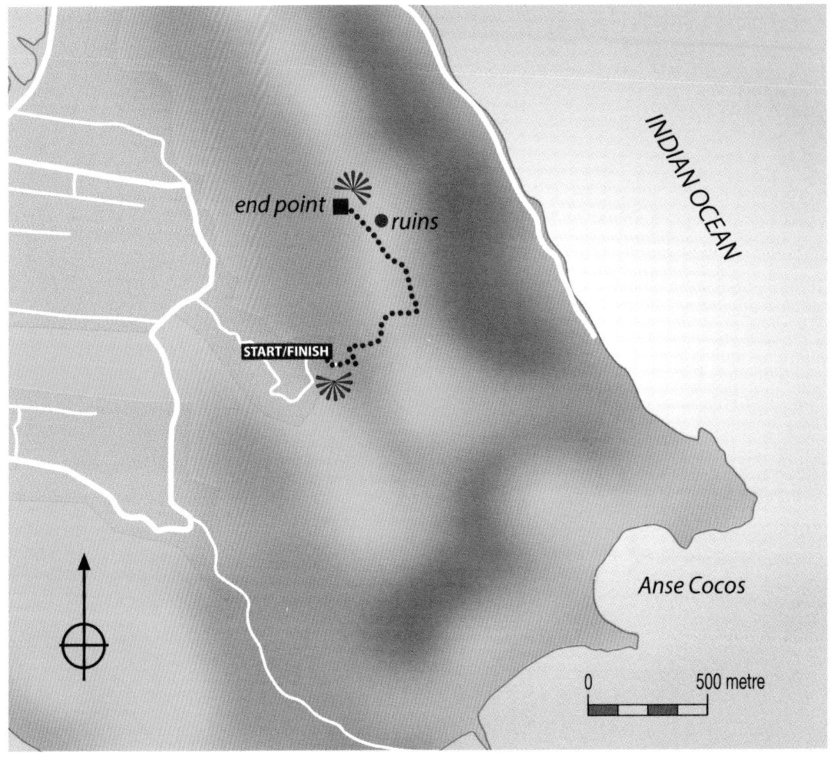

out for the Seychelles Bulbul with its distinctive call. Once you reach the top, the Nid D'Aigle path continues to the left along the plateau, eventually reaching an antenna next to a concrete building. To your right you will see the island of Félicité in the distance.

Keep going through another small section of forest, where you will find the ruins of an old village. The final ascent takes you back out into the open until you reach the summit at 333m. Once on top of the glacis, you are greeted by uninterrupted views of the surrounding islands, including Praslin, Marianne, Petite Soeur and Grande Soeur.

The return journey is back down the same path and does not take long. Once you reach the Belle Vue restaurant, you can stop for a cold drink and a bite to eat while you take in the incredible view one last time.

Veuve Special Reserve trail

A SERIES OF WELL-MAINTAINED PATHS THROUGH LOWLAND FOREST, HOME TO THE SEYCHELLES BLACK PARADISE FLYCATCHER

Level Beginner
Distance 1 km
Time 30 minutes
Getting there By bicycle from La Passe, follow the road south until you come to a junction, turn left and the reserve will be on your left-hand side .

Located on the western side of the island, the Veuve Special Reserve covers 0.078km² of forest plateau. The reserve is managed by the Seychelles Parks and Gardens Authority and is open from Monday to Friday at 8 a.m. to 4 p.m. At the time of writing, for non-residents, the entry fee is SR150 for unguided tours, or SR200 for guided. As the trail is flat and there are plenty of places where you can sit down and rest, a trip to the Veuve is suitable for people of all abilities.

Getting to the reserve is easy by bicycle, and there is an area where you can leave your bike outside the entrance near the visitor centre. Inside the reserve there are a number of well-maintained paths, and although it does not take long to complete the nature trail, it is possible to spend hours sitting on one of the benches in the forest.

The reserve was created to provide a protected breeding and feeding habitat for the endemic Seychelles Black Paradise Flycatcher. The species is currently listed on the IUCN Red List of Endangered Species as Vulnerable due to habitat loss, and in recent years birds have been translocated to Denis and Curieuse Islands as part of an ongoing conservation programme. There are six breeding territories in the reserve, and it is fairly easy to spot both males and females. The latter have a chestnut plumage with a white belly and black head, while the males are entirely black with distinctive long tail feathers. Look out for the nests, which are built on low-hanging branches, often close to the paths. The Alexandrian Laurel and Indian Almond are the preferred tree species. Aside from the flycatchers, it is possible to see other endemics, including the Seychelles Sunbird and Seychelles Bulbul, while the wetlands in the reserve are home to mud terrapins, primarily the Black Mud Terrapin.

A female Seychelles Paradise Flycatcher sits on her nest near the path.

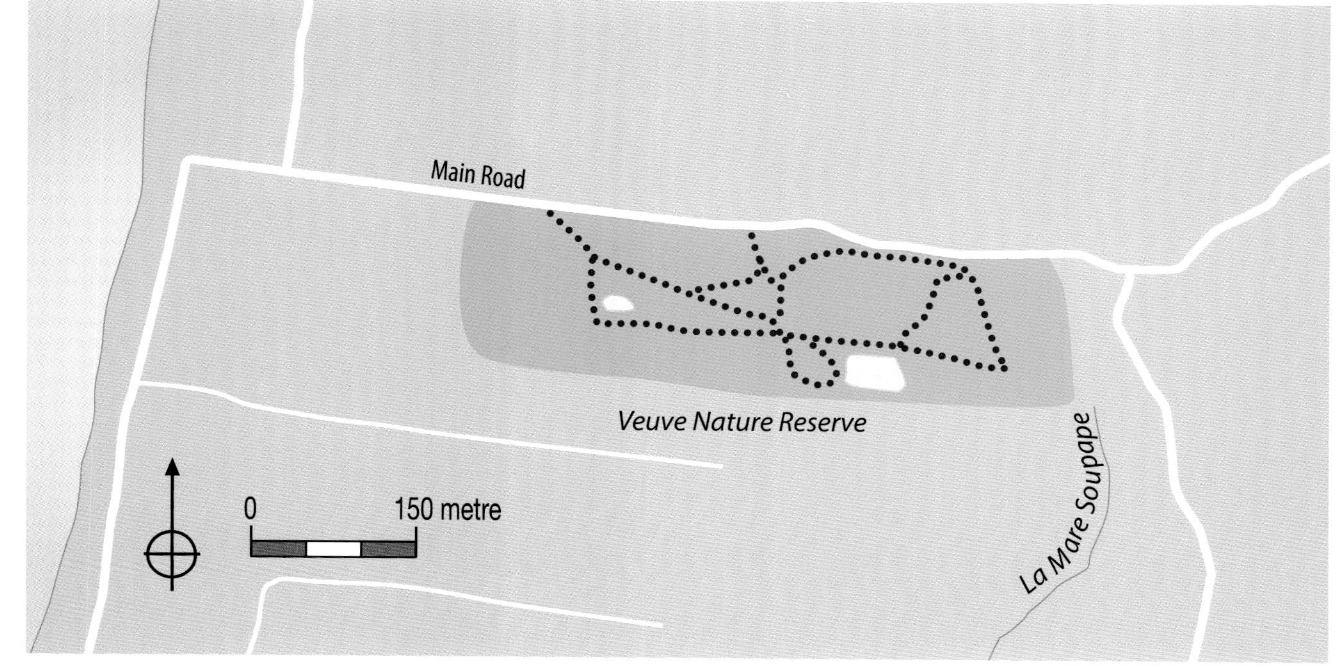
Main Road
Veuve Nature Reserve
0
150 metre
La Mare Soupape

CURIEUSE ISLAND

Curieuse is the fifth largest of the granitic islands, and its surrounding waters make up the Curieuse Marine National Park, which is under the management of the Seychelles Parks and Gardens Authority. The island is accessed by taking a boat from Anse Volbert on Praslin. Day trips can be arranged through hotels and guest houses, or by approaching one of the taxi-boat operators on the beach. The island is open to visitors until 5 p.m. and day packages can be purchased, which include national park fees and a barbecue lunch.

Lacking in roads and with little infrastructure, Curieuse is navigated through paths cut into the mountainside and along boardwalks in the mangroves. There is a coastal plateau dominated by Alexandrian Laurel at Anse Jose, where you can find ruins from the old colony of leprosy patients and the doctor's house (a museum that provides information on the old colony and the history of Curieuse Island). Tour operators often bring visitors here, as there are also a barbecue area, toilets and shower facilities. The park rangers have their station at Baie Larie, a beautiful bay situated to the east of Anse Jose. This is the best place to see giant tortoises and includes the tortoise nursery. Away from the plateaux of Anse Jose and Baie Laraie, the island is very dry. Curieuse is the only island other than Praslin to have a wild population of Coco-de-mer, and these iconic trees are scattered throughout the island. However, due to the poor quality of the soil and the dry conditions, the trees tend not to grow as tall as those found within the Vallée de Mai.

 View of the old turtle pond and Baie Laraie, Curieuse Island.

Anse Badamier trail

VISIT A REMOTE BEACH ON THE WILD NORTHERN COAST OF CURIEUSE ISLAND

Level Beginner
Distance 3.6km (return trip)
Time 2 hours
Getting there By taxi-boat from Praslin.

Most tourists visiting Curieuse Island walk along the mangrove boardwalk, visit the island's southern beaches or spend time with the giant tortoises at the park rangers' station. However, for those looking to get away from the crowds, the Anse Badamier trail offers the perfect escape.

Beginning at Baie Laraie, and facing away from the sea, the path starts at the base of a rocky outcrop on the left-hand side of the beach, and rises over a small glacis before joining the mangrove boardwalk. Continue along the boardwalk, looking out for juvenile Lemon Sharks among the mangrove roots, until you reach an intersection with a sign directing you towards Anse Badamier. Take a right towards Anse Badamier, passing through the mangroves and picking up the trail as it ascends through glacis lined with the introduced Cocoplum. When you reach the top of the glacis, you are greeted with a view of the ocean and Aride Island in the distance. It

The wooden walkway through the mangroves.

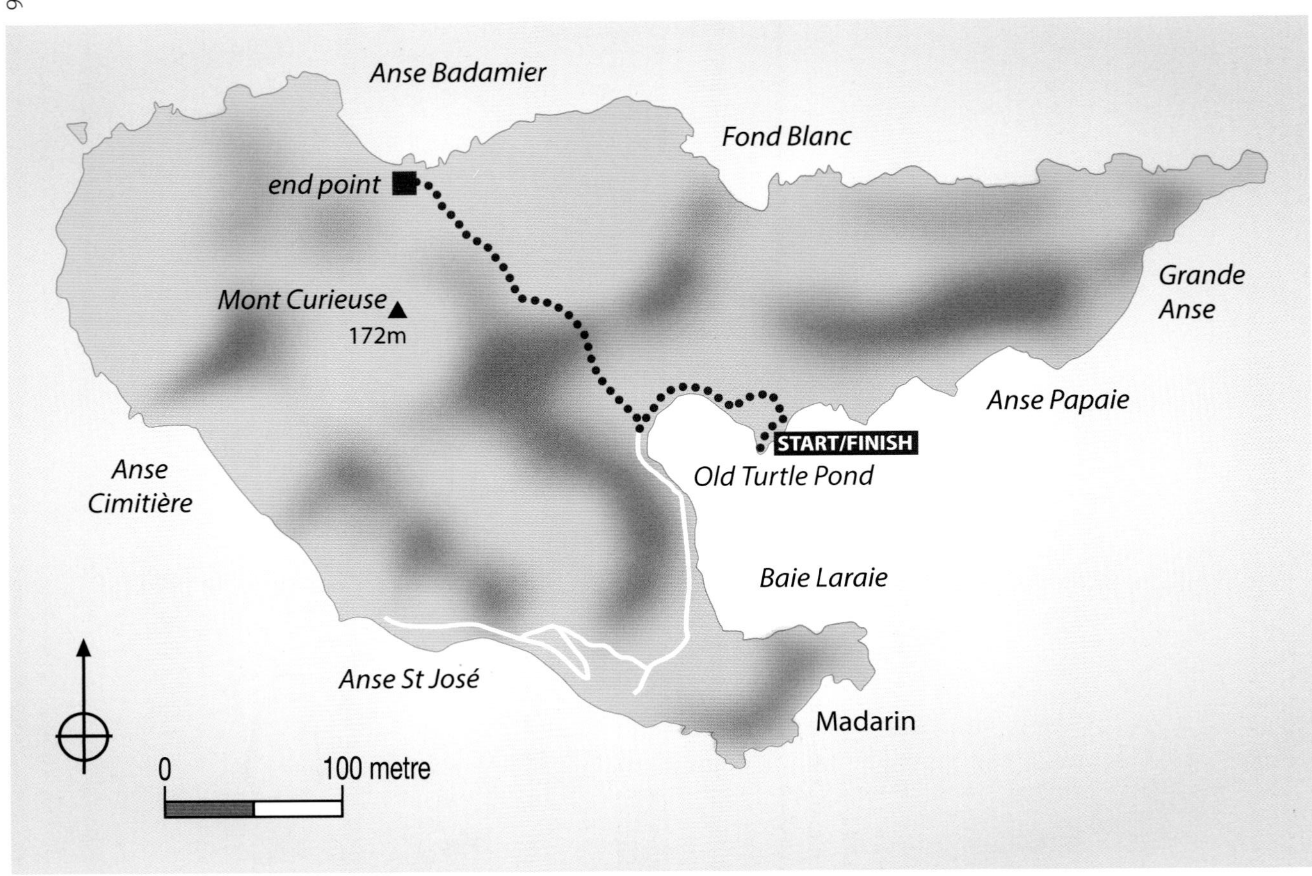
Anse Badamier
Fond Blanc
end point
Mont Curieuse
172m
Grande
Anse
Anse Papaie
START/FINISH
Old Turtle Pond
Anse
Cimitière
Baie Laraie
Anse St José
Madarin
0
100 metre

View of Anse Badamier with Aride Island in the distance.

is also possible to see Coco-de-mer trees on the hillside. From here it is another 30 minutes to Badamier beach.

The 200m stretch of beach is lined with Coconut trees and it is likely that you will have it to yourself, making it feel like your very own piece of paradise. Depending on the time of year, the sea can be rough at Anse Badamier. However, if the conditions are calm, there is excellent snorkelling to be had among the numerous granite rocks that rise up from the shallow water. Look out for schools of parrotfish, Whitetip Reef Sharks and Hawksbill Turtles.

The return journey is back along the same path until you reach the intersection at the mangroves. From here you can either return to Baie Laraie, or carry on to Anse Jose, where your taxi-boat can collect you to head back to Praslin.

Granite boulders on Anse Badamier.

ARIDE ISLAND

Aride Island Special Reserve is the most northerly of the Seychelles granitic islands and is located 9km north of Praslin. The island is 1.6km long and covers an area of approximately 0.68km^2. There is a single beach, which runs for 800m on the south side of the island, while the island's northern coast is dominated by steep cliffs that rise to 134m above sea level.

Aride Island is managed by the Island Conservation Society.

Declared a Special Reserve in 1979, Aride has been managed by the Island Conservation Society (ICS) since 2001. The island is characterized by native woodland, granite outcrops and a freshwater marsh. It is best known for its bird life, with Aride being one of the most important seabird islands in the western Indian Ocean. The world's largest populations of Tropical Shearwaters and Lesser Noddies are both found on Aride, while a small number of Red-tailed Tropicbirds also breed here, making it the only place to observe

Frigatebirds are a common sight around Aride Island.

Wright's Gardenia is endemic to the island of Aride.

these birds within the granitic island group. The island is also home to thousands of non-breeding frigatebirds (both Lesser and Greater).

Endemic land birds are well represented, and it is possible to see the Seychelles Fody, Seychelles Warbler, Seychelles Magpie Robin, Seychelles Blue Pigeon and Seychelles Sunbird without too much difficulty.

Access to the island is by boat and is weather dependent. The island is usually open to visitors from Monday to Friday between September and May, and day trips can be booked through the ICS. At the time of writing, the entrance fee is SR650 for adults and SR300 for children (4–13 years). Small boats usually depart for Aride from Grand Anse on Praslin in the mornings, and the journey takes about 45 minutes. On arriving at the island you receive an orientation before setting off on a professionally guided nature tour, which lasts about two hours. The tour takes you from the lowland plateau and the human settlement, through native forest where you will see Wright's Skink and the Seychelles Skink, both of which are present in high numbers. It has been said that Aride has the highest density of lizards anywhere on the planet.

Continuing upwards along the trail you also encounter Wright's Gardenia, which occurs naturally only on Aride. When you are more than 100m above sea level, you eventually reach the end of the trail and a clearing with views of the impressive cliffs and the ocean below. This area is home to the frigatebird roost and you may see hundreds of these impressive birds circling in the sky around you.

The tour ends back down at the visitor centre, where you are able to rest, go for a swim or explore a little further until it is time to leave and return to Praslin.

COUSIN ISLAND

Cousin Island Special Reserve is located 2km from Praslin Island. The 0.29km^2 granite island is managed by Nature Seychelles, a local NGO, and is open to the public Monday to Friday. Visitors' fees contribute towards the management of the reserve, including research and conservation projects. At the time of writing, the entrance fee is SR600 for non-residents. Cousin is accessed by a short 15-minute boat trip from Grande Anse on neighbouring Praslin Island.

Once on the island you are given a guided tour by one of the wardens, which usually lasts about 75 minutes. Although it is small in size, Cousin boasts an abundance of native and endemic wildlife. The island was previously dominated by a Coconut plantation, but has since been transformed through habitat restoration and the removal of invasive species. Today it is dominated by native forest, including Pisonia. The sticky seeds of the Pisonia tree cling to the feathers of seabirds, allowing them to be dispersed widely, but are often detrimental to the seabirds.

Tours usually focus on the plateau, taking in the forest and marsh area, although depending on the size and the physical ability of the group, they may also visit some of the hillier sections of the island.

Highlights include encounters with giant tortoises in the forest, as well sightings of the Seychelles Magpie Robin. Other endemic land birds to be found on Cousin include the Seychelles Fody, Seychelles Blue Pigeon, Seychelles Warbler and Seychelles Sunbird.

 The view of Praslin from the top of Cousin Island.

An Aldabra Giant Tortoise cools down in Cousin's wetland.

Because it is a rat-free island, Cousin is a haven for nesting seabirds, and the Tropical Shearwater, Wedge-tailed Shearwater, Bridled Tern, Lesser Noddy, Brown Noddy, White-tailed Tropicbird and White Tern all nest on the island.

Following the tour, there is time to relax and take a stroll along the beach before you leave the island. Cousin is one of the most important Hawksbill Turtle nesting sites in the Seychelles granitic islands, and encounters with turtles on the island's beaches are common during the nesting season. The island hosts the largest population of nesting Hawksbill Turtles of the granitic islands.

A young Bridled Tern calls for its parents.

References

FURTHER READING

Mason-Parker, C. & Walton, R. 2015, 2020. *Underwater Guide to Seychelles.* John Beaufoy Publishing, Oxford, UK.

Mason-Parker, C. & Daniels, J. 2015. *Underwater Eden.* John Beaufoy Publishing, Oxford, UK.

Mason-Parker, C., Daly, R., Keating, C. & Stevens, G. 2021. *Reef Fishes of Seychelles.* John Beaufoy Publishing, Oxford, UK.

Hill, M. & Currie, D. 2007. *Wildlife of Seychelles.* HarperCollins Publishers Ltd, London, UK.

Hansen, S. & Laboudallon, V. 2016. *Flora of the Seychelles. A Field Guide to Selected Plants.* Denmark.

Rocamora, G. & Henriette, E. 2015. *Invasive Alien Species in Seychelles.* Muséum National d'Histoire Naturelle, Paris, France.

Skerret, A. & Disley, T. 2011. *Birds of Seychelles.* Bloomsbury Publishing PLC, London, UK.

Skerret, A. 2015. *A Photo Guide to the Birds of Seychelles.* Camerapix, Nairobi, Kenya.

WEBSITES

Archipelago Images www.archipelagoimages.net
Green Islands Foundation greenislandsfoundation.blogspot.com
Island Conservation Society www.islandconservationseychelles.com
Marine Conservation Society Seychelles www.mcss.sc
Nature Seychelles www.natureseychelles.org
Seychelles Islands Foundation www.sif.sc
Seychelles Parks & Gardens Authority www.snpa.gov.sc
Seychelles Plant Gallery www.seychellesplantgallery.com

ACKNOWLEDGEMENTS

The author would like to thank all those who contributed to the making of *A Photographic Guide to the Wildlife of Seychelles.* The creation of such a book would not have been possible without the valuable knowledge, insight and feedback of numerous individuals, whose essential contributions were all very valuable to producing the finished guide.

Particular thanks must go to the photographers who provided images of species, and to Rebecca Loustau-Lalanne and Dr Jeanne Mortimer for taking the time to review the text.

INDEX

FLORA